Praise for
# The Cul-de-Sac Syndrome
*Turning Around the Unsustainable American Dream*

## by John F. Wasik

"John Wasik's *The Cul-de-Sac Syndrome* offers enough to chew on for three sets of teeth, enough to digest for three stomachs and then alerts the mind faster than an approaching siren."

> **— RALPH NADER**
> Consumer advocate

"Wow! Get ready for a totally original look at the American dream. Yes, we slipped off track. Now we need real solutions. And fast. Here they are. Wasik delivers the first truly multidisciplinary examination—using psychology, planning, law, architecture, and history to focus on working solutions that get us back on track and keep the American dream alive for future generations. This is a must-read winner!"

> **— PAUL B. FARRELL, JD, PhD**
> Columnist, MarketWatch.com
> Author, *The Millionaire Code*

"As John Wasik eloquently writes in his new book, *The Cul-De-Sac Syndrome,* quoting national statistics to describe the most local of all markets—the residential real estate market—almost misses the point. This excellent book takes a ground-level look at the causes of our housing crisis and offers a myriad of ideas on reinventing the concepts of home and community."

> **— ILYCE R. GLINK**
> Syndicated real estate columnist
> Author, *100 Questions Every First-Time Home Buyer Should Ask*
> Publisher, ThinkGlink.com

"*The Cul-De-Sac Syndrome* is a genuine kick to the head, showing how our individual quests for the biggest house on the hill is destroying our environment, the economy, and our physical and mental health. But *The Cul-de-Sac Syndrome* is no dead end. It offers a new, green, urbanized promised land with real community, more free time, and a higher living standard. It's a masterful blueprint to unpave paradise and restore the world we cherish."

> **— LAURENCE KOTLIKOFF**
> Professor of Economics, Boston University
> Coauthor of *Spend 'Til the End: The Revolutionary Guide to Raising Your Living Standard—Today and When You Retire*

# The
# CUL-DE-SAC
## Syndrome

Also by
**John F. Wasik**

*The Audacity of Help:*
*Obama's Economic Plan and the Remaking of America*

Also available from
**Bloomberg Press**

*Aqua Shock:*
*The Water Crisis in America*
by Susan J. Marks

*Collateral Damaged:*
*The Marketing of Consumer Debt to America*
by Charles R. Geisst

*Pension Dumping:*
*The Reasons, the Wreckage, the Stakes for Wall Street*
by Fran Hawthorne

A complete list of our titles is available at
**www.bloomberg.com/books**

# The
# CUL-DE-SAC
## Syndrome

Turning Around the Unsustainable
American Dream

JOHN F. WASIK

BLOOMBERG PRESS

NEW YORK

First edition published 2009

1 3 5 7 9 10 8 6 4 2

Library of Congress Cataloging-in-Publication Data

Wasik, John F.
The cul-de-sac syndrome : turning around the unsustainable American dream / John Wasik.
    p. cm.
    Includes bibliographical references and index.
    Summary: "The Cul-de-Sac Syndrome explores why homeownership has become a fractured dream and presents ways to revive it. Combining analysis with insights into cultural and economic myths, the book provides an incisive look at the consequences of unsustainable lifestyle, exposing its economic, cultural, and market-related roots and the larger effects on the community, economy, and environment"—Provided by publisher.
    ISBN 978-1-57660-320-8 (alk. paper)
    1. Home ownership—United States. 2. Housing development—United States. 3. Sustainable development—United States. I. Title.

HD7287.82.U6W37 2009
333.33'80973—dc22

2009002103

To my father, Arthur Stanley Wasik

# Contents

# Preface

HOW DID THE UNITED STATES succumb to one of the most devastating housing recessions since the 1930s? Weren't homes supposed to be the safest investments on the planet? Ultimately, the housing bust may turn out to be one of the biggest financial blowups in history, rivaling the Great Depression with more than $4 trillion in wealth evaporating. Millions entered a financial dead end during this period of irrational exuberance. It may take years for them to escape from it.

What drove this flood of exuberant optimism? Did everyone from mortgage brokers to Wall Street simply get greedy? Or do the true causes lie much deeper, in the American dream itself and in the goal that eventually became an obsession with ever-bigger homes? A bubble in which demand exceeded realistic economic fundamentals was triggered by a number of uniquely American cultural values, desires, and economic shortcomings. These underlying reasons for the debacle have been ingrained in Western culture for almost half a millennium. They're myths that have flourished precisely at a time when Americans' view of themselves, their post-9/11 security, and their shaky financial future were being tested as never before.

The stereotypical villains in the subprime story have been Wall Street bankers, the government, and greedy participants, from speculating "flippers" to the Federal Reserve. There's plenty of blame to spread around when it comes to who was motivated by pure avarice or criminal exploitation, and much of that picture has been illuminated. Those who thought they would profit handsomely have already been exposed, have taken their losses, and are known to anyone following this calamity. It's far too easy, though, to point fingers at the purveyors of human excesses. That's only part of the story.

The American dream—and what it has cost us—is what underlies the crisis and what this book explores. How did we come to believe that a home should be an investment worth enough to propel millions to leverage beyond their ability to pay? In an age of burgeoning info-technology, why are we still building homes with the latest *nineteenth-century* techniques? What was the market behavior that drove homeowners into subprime loans and moving ever farther away from jobs and cities? How did we come up with the idea that we should buy as much house as we can afford, with no regard for the cost of heating and cooling it and the time and expense of getting to it?

We've gotten stuck in a vicious cycle, a cul-de-sac of unsustainable costs and serious long-term consequences for our health and our environment. After following the bubble and its aftermath since 2001 as a personal finance columnist for Bloomberg News, I've gained some insights into urban planning, resource depletion, and homebuilding techniques and economics that cast a critical—and disturbing—light on the American dream of homeownership. That dream led to the creation of what I call "spurbs," the car-dependent sprawling urban areas, unconnected to core cities by public transportation and beset by unsustainable costs for infrastructure, services, and resources. As highly leveraged locations ravaged by foreclosures and falling property values, these enclaves will hurt the most in coming years.

We've suffered from a cul-de-sac syndrome on not only how to finance the American dream, but how to build it in the future so that it's economically and ecologically sustainable. How do we cure this malady, one that's responsible for global financial calamity? Even if the home market fully recovers with higher prices, home starts, and sales, the deep-seated problems this shortsighted cultural mythology brought about will haunt future generations if we don't correct them.

I've traveled from coast to coast several times to highlight the myriad stories of innovators, dreamers, activists, and visionaries who are still creatively searching for a way to make the American dream attainable and affordable. I've consulted with the leading minds in architecture, economics, engineering, homebuilding, and urban planning to uncover insights on the past, present, and future of the home market.

Readdressing, reimagining, and redesigning the foundation of the American dream has no downside because we will be creating and preserving jobs and wealth and even addressing global warming. In the words of John Ruskin, "That country is the richest which nourishes the greatest number of noble and happy human beings; that man is richest, who, having perfected the functions of his own life to the utmost, has also the widest helpful influence, both personal, and by means of his possessions, over the lives of others." It all starts in our homes and communities—my home, your home.

# Introduction
## The Foundation Cracks

THE LAST SPANISH SULTAN, Boabdil, sobbed as he left the Alhambra. His heart was broken as he looked back upon the heavenly complex of crenulated arches, fountains, and pools within the splendid palaces of the Moorish rulers of Granada in southern Spain, on his way to exile in Africa in 1492. He was not only mourning the loss of his bastion to the Catholic monarchs Ferdinand and Isabella but also grieving for what might have been—a culturally vivacious state where no group had to supplant the other due to lack of land or resources. Although there was certainly barbarism during and after the Alhambra's golden age, the combined will of the houses of Castile and Aragon set in motion a land lust that would ravage two continents.

Christopher Columbus had met with Queen Isabella in the newly conquered Alhambra, and he had his marching orders. Gold and land were the primary objectives of the Spanish crown. They had coffers to fill, armadas to build, and conquistadors to finance. Keeping everything in check was their form of the Gestapo—the Inquisition. Jews or Moors who would not convert to Christianity were tortured or killed. Even if they were baptized, they were subject to abuse and discrimination. Jews, who had contributed immeasurably during the halcyon days of the Alhambra, were eventually exiled.

As strangers in a strange land, the Moors were the most successful diplomats on the Iberian peninsula, building their dominion over a seven-hundred-year period. During their tenure, they practiced tolerance, translated the great works of antiquity from Greek into Arabic and Latin, and then entreated Europe to feast on the knowledge and imagination of

1

the classical authors. Pythagoras, Ptolemy, Aristotle, and the great theo-
reticians of ethics, physics, and philosophy were reborn in the learning
enclaves of Toledo and Córdoba. Andalusia became the Harvard, Princeton, and Yale of Western civilization from the eighth century through the
fifteenth. Establishing a multicultural ministate on a peninsula that had
been invaded by Celts, Romans, Franks, and Visigoths, the Moors had
few peers in the realm of cultural sustainability in their heyday.

## A Housing Crisis and a Fractured Dream

Ever since anyone can remember, most Americans, including millions who
arrived on these shores as strangers, have wanted their own Alhambras in
shining cities on a hill. "A man's home is his castle," the old expression
goes, dating back to the height of the Spanish empire. Yet at the time I
was exploring the Spanish palace complex, millions of Americans were
about to lose their citadels. A period in which nearly 70 percent of Americans were able to own homes was about to end as dramatically as the sultan's life in his palace. A new era of recrimination and economic loss on a
scale that had not been seen since the Great Depression was beginning.

By the time the housing bust sucked the air out of the stock market
in 2008, the *New York Times* had trumpeted a front-page headline
that read "Housing Woes in U.S. Spread Around the Globe." The U.S.
home market was in a vicious recession and the general economy was
on the brink, too. In the most expensive areas for homeownership—
far-away places where Americans moved so that they could afford their
Alhambras—the economic strain was like a dam that had been breached.
A half a trillion dollars in adjustable mortgages would be resetting
through 2009; that is, their monthly payments would likely rise to unaffordable levels. Those unable to refinance would be forced into foreclosure. Some 60 percent of those loan holders were in California, where
purchasing the basic American home was the costliest proposition in the
United States. Other places—Chicago, Cleveland, Detroit, Miami—
were feeling acute pain, too.

How did the American dream turn into such a crushing, unsustainable debt burden? Populists blame Wall Street. Conservatives blame
greedy, underfinanced homeowners. Liberals cite the lack of regulation
in lending and securities markets. As I followed this developing crisis—
indeed, I warned about it in my Bloomberg News column as early as

2002—only one thing is certain: The debacle had been brewing for *centuries* and has intimate ties to a cultural obsession. The great bubble in home prices was not only economically unsustainable, it revealed some deep-seated ecological, social, and public health woes. To understand how this downturn unfolded, we need to examine what I call the "cul-de-sac syndrome," a combination of some of the more glaring financial and cultural ailments that have led us to a dead end in private American housing.

## Devaluing Castles: Inside a $10 Trillion Debacle

Spain is five thousand miles and eight months away as I glance at the latest headlines on my Bloomberg terminal, my ever-vigilant connection to the colossus of global finance. Forecasts on how much the housing market will decline in the long run range from 30 percent to 50 percent. Places like Boston, Chicago, New York, and Seattle were relatively unscathed but still are glutted with unsold homes, apartments, and condos. About 80 percent of the nation's houses declined in value in 2008 in the top one hundred largest markets. This was the steepest decline in residential property prices in a generation. When the housing market peaked in late 2006, few could envision its global devastation from Shanghai to Frankfurt. The resulting credit crunch strangled bond and stock markets and triggered a massive recession that began in 2007. Unemployment soared from Wall Street to Main Street. The idea that a home was a solid investment for eternity has become a cruel footnote to early twenty-first-century history.

The housing cataclysm will rival the Great Depression in terms of its economic damage and will redefine the journey known as the American dream. Imagine the largest, most valuable ship in the world carrying the equivalent of most of U.S. home equity, stock values, and mortgage securities hitting a reef and spewing its cargo into the sea; some $10 trillion may be lost. Banks that had invested in this ship wrote down about $1 trillion in losses. The government flotilla that mounted the rescue and recovery pledged $8.5 trillion (and counting) to fix the disaster. That's more than the gross domestic products of China, India, and Canada (as of 2008).

The ship started out charting a very different course: *Everyone* could make money owning, selling, or financing an American home. Anyone could be a real estate entrepreneur. The traditional rules of supply and demand, historical price increases, and creditworthiness were thrown out the window of high and low finance during this age of "froth," which is how Federal Reserve Chairman Alan Greenspan described the housing market at its height. This epic understatement ignored the fraudulent reality of the bubble when credit ratings agencies rated junk mortgage securities "AAA," real estate appraisers vastly overvalued properties, and mortgage sellers freely handed out money to anyone with a few blood cells. Stories like the one about the migrant strawberry picker with $14,000 of annual income getting a mortgage for a $720,000 home were common. If you could sign your name, you got credit, because the mantra of this bacchanal was "home prices only go up."

Much of the catastrophe was blamed on greedy Wall Street bankers, mortgage brokers, compromised appraisers, mortgage fraud artists, and aggressive speculators, also known as "flippers." What has received little attention is the culture that lit the fuse to this explosion: the hallowed good intentions of the American ideal, the sacred goal of homeownership, and the fallacy that house values never fall. Millions had bet wrongly on these misconceptions. The violent economic reality was that millions couldn't afford this promise in the face of ever-lower after-inflation wages, reduced benefits, and devastated 401(k) balances in the aftermath of the 1990s dot-com meltdown. Homes were overpriced and beyond the financial reach of far too many Americans (and Europeans as well). No savings? No problem! Everyone qualified for a mortgage in the age of froth.

Did anyone see this coming? A few prophets spoke up, but the sternest warnings were ignored even as powerful money moguls like Ben Bernanke and Alan Greenspan at the Federal Reserve knew it was happening. When the bubbles were inflating, regulators and bond-rating agencies—like the bumbling cop Inspector Clouseau—looked the other way. More obvious scoundrels were the mortgage brokers, predatory loan sharks, bankers, and Wall Street financial engineering sharpies who took their fees as the riskiest junk mortgages were sold to the highest bidders.

Who enabled these financial purveyors? Just about anyone who wanted to buy, sell, finance, or build a house. An overriding cultural ethos promoted homeownership at any cost. Everyone from President George W. Bush to a massive combine of government and private interests had a stake in promoting home buying. After all, a key rite of ascension into the middle class was buying a home. Millions felt that they were entitled to the symbolic status of one's castle.

## The Unattainable Home

Even before the home bubble burst, homes cost too much for more than four out of ten Americans. Only 56 percent of Americans could afford a modestly priced home in 2002, the first full year of the bubble. And as Americans went deeper into debt to finance their dream, they accumulated less and less of a tangible ownership stake. Home equity as a percentage of market value peaked in 1982—at 70 percent—after a brutal recession. More than half of American homeowners with a mortgage would *owe* more than they owned at the end of 2008. About 7.5 million were spending more than half of their income on housing costs.

The craving for upward mobility through home ownership escalated even as families on the edge of "making it" were falling behind economically. The think tank Demos said that 23 million families became "economically insecure" from 2000 to 2006, while 4 million experienced economic decline. This erosion in prosperity was triggered by a 22 percent decline in financial assets (following the dot-com bust), loss of health benefits, and an overall rise in the cost of homeownership (up 9 percent during that period). The reaction to this backsliding—buying a home as an investment—was the equivalent of a couple on the verge of divorce deciding to have a child in hopes that it would save their marriage. For more than 3 million in or facing foreclosure in 2009, this thinking proved financially catastrophic.

The housing bust represents a profound loss of wealth since few households had significant savings outside of their homes, as values dropped to a median $200,000 in early 2009 from $221,900 at the height of the bubble in 2006. In California, always on the fault line between profound innovation and multiple disasters, the boom and bust was a tragic manic-depressive episode. The median home price in Southern California alone slid to $285,000 by the end of 2008, 44 percent below the peak of $505,000 in 2007. Although the decline allowed more people to afford homes, even during the bust only one-fifth of Los Angeles residents could afford the median-priced home—up from 2 percent during the boom.

## The Bust's Fallout

The housing bust created a firestorm of collateral damage.

➤ Lehman Brothers, one of the oldest and most venerable investment banks, was forced into bankruptcy and liquidation during a run on its assets in the late summer and fall of 2008. Its subprime mortgage and credit default swap holdings were essentially to blame, creating the largest business bankruptcy in U.S. history. Its demise released a tsunami of securities- and derivatives-related demons. Basically, when home prices collapsed, the value of the securities holding mortgages also went south. These "toxic assets" imperiled any institution that held them.

➤ When the run commenced on Lehman, it drove Merrill Lynch, the country's largest brokerage house, into the arms of Bank of America, creating the world's largest brokerage with more than $2.5 trillion in assets and 20,000 "financial advisers." Merrill, whose symbol was an optimistic though ferocious black bull, had also invested billions in tainted subprime securities. Government regulators also forced the sale of Bear Stearns Companies, another major mortgage securities player, to JPMorgan Chase for a bargain-basement sale price of $10 a share (the initial price was $2 a share). Like Lehman, Bear effectively evaporated.

➤ The U.S. government seized Freddie Mac and Fannie Mae, the two largest mortgage issuers and guarantors, and promised to infuse the companies with cash to keep them afloat. Their liabilities vastly exceeded their assets and they were losing a total $50 billion in the third quarter of 2008 alone. Since they insured, loaned, or sold securities representing $5 trillion—about half of the U.S. mortgage market—they were deemed "too big to fail."

➤ Caught in the opaque business of insuring mortgage securities through the shadowy and then-unregulated world of credit default insurance, the government effectively took over AIG, the world's largest insurer. The Federal Reserve lent it more than $80 billion by early 2009, part of a $150 billion bailout. It, too, was deemed too large to go bust, because its mortgage and derivatives positions threatened the global financial system.

➤ Seeking refuge in the regulated banking system, the remaining Wall Street investment banks morphed into old-fashioned, deposit-oriented banks. Goldman Sachs and Morgan Stanley applied to become regulated banking companies with federal oversight. American Express followed later in the year. The Age of Froth was truly over as the cowboy operations that thrived on 30-to-1 (and higher) leverage became history.

➤ The mother of all bailouts came as wintry storms arrived with an Old Testament vengeance in the autumn of 2008. With rancorous and reluctant Congressional approval, Treasury Secretary Henry Paulson and Fed Chairman Ben Bernanke on October 1 ushered through a sketchy $700 billion bailout package called the Troubled Asset Relief Program (TARP), which would pump money into banks, possibly buy bad mortgages, and prop up the financial system for a short time. This massive cash transfusion was designed to prevent credit markets from shutting down and avert a global depression. Meanwhile, the Fed was lending some $2 trillion to banks, attempting to break a credit freeze that threatened to shut down all institutional lending. Paulson later backtracked on his earlier proposal to buy mortgages, triggering even more concerns that his master plan was ill conceived and ineptly managed. Sensing that the real purpose of all of the bailout measures was to stem the foreclosure crisis, the Federal Deposit Insurance Corporation announced its own mortgage bailout plan on the heels of the Paulson announcement. Several large banks said they would do voluntary loan modifications to reduce the cost of adjustable-rate loans, although they were under no legal obligation to do so.

➤ After more dithering over how TARP funds would be allocated, Secretary Paulson and Fed Chairman Bernanke moved to prop up Citigroup, one of the largest global lenders, with a $20 billion cash infusion and guarantee of more than $300 billion of its loans. Within days, responding to criticism that banks were the exclusive benefactors of the government's bailout, the Fed moved to guarantee certain mortgage, credit-card, and student-loan securities.

## Enter Obama

Although the Barack Obama administration-in-waiting moved quickly following the election by announcing its economic team and various stimulus proposals, it was clear the calamity hadn't subsided nor had

Congress finished adding economic incentives of its own. Obama's team, consisting of former New York Federal Reserve Bank President Timothy Geithner (Treasury secretary), former Treasury Secretary Lawrence Summers (National Economic Council head), and former Federal Reserve Chairman Paul Volcker (chairman, Economic Recovery Advisory Board), were given immediate marching orders to halt the carnage left from the housing bust. Even as the lame-duck Congress and the failed Bush administration threw every resource possible at the crisis (including a flimsy cash handout to General Motors, Ford, and Chrysler), it seemed intractable going into 2009. Home prices had fallen the most on record through the end of 2008 with an eighteen-month supply of houses sitting unsold. Since none of the myriad bailout measures had shut down foreclosures, the number of people defaulting on their mortgages continued to rise. The U.S. home market remained hobbled.

Obama's actions reflected widespread concerns that the global economy was on the brink of repeating the horrors of 1930, when fear dominated every market across the world. Although it was necessary that Congress stem the crisis and fortunate that it did with its relatively swift actions of late September and early October 2008, it acted with almost no meaningful oversight of who was getting taxpayer funds and why. Bloomberg News had to file a federal lawsuit to obtain the list of banks receiving $2 *trillion* in Fed loans. It wasn't clear how AIG was spending its bailout funds nor were there any strings attached to the money given to major banks. Meanwhile, it wasn't clear whether any of the massive realignments on Wall Street or the various Washington bailout measures would halt the pace of foreclosures, get buyers back into the market, or drastically reshape the U.S. housing market. It may take years for the most troubled markets to recover, barring an aggressive program to shut down foreclosures and jump-start home buying.

## The Causes

What triggered this fool's-gold rush and subsequent crash? When prices peaked in July 2005, the torrent of new adjustable loans—often provided with little or no credit or income verification—hit a wall when the bubble burst. Wall Street also stopped buying and bundling these mortgages into exotic vehicles called "collateralized debt obligations" and into other vehicles, which dried up the supply of cheap money greasing the home-finance machine. New home sales fell more than 60 percent from that summit. The great, sure-thing investment of American homes, which in the new century had been outperforming everything save for corporate bonds, commodities, and preferred stocks—things middle Americans didn't really understand—got abandoned by Wall Street the same way the money men lost interest in telecommunication stocks in 2000. They discovered how much risk was concentrated in their pools of mortgage securities and fled the toxic debt like people running from a burning building.

Once the easy money from Wall Street dried up, the bad news on Main Street got worse by the day. By November of 2007, home prices dropped in thirteen of the twenty largest markets surveyed for the S&P/Case-Shiller home price index, reaching "another grim milestone," according to Robert Shiller, the Yale Law School professor who co-created the index and who would become the Jeremiah of the housing bust.

As 2008 dawned, double-digit declines continued. The leaders in losses were Las Vegas, Miami, and Phoenix, each posting about 20 percent drops in year-over-year prices. Southern California was well represented, with San Diego and Los Angeles showing 16 percent dips. Detroit, Tampa, San Francisco, Washington (DC), and Minneapolis rounded out the list. All but one of the cities—Charlotte, North Carolina—was on the list of losers.

While home prices were falling like meteorites, new home sales plunged 30 percent in February, the lowest level in thirteen years. Builders struggled to sell off some of their inventories, offering low-rate financing and free upgrades in kitchens and baths. Several went bankrupt as it became clear it would take more than throwing in a granite countertop to sell homes in this kind of market. With more than 4.5 million unsold homes on the market, there were virtually no buyers, and the sellers who were holding out for top-of-the-bubble prices weren't able to move their properties. More than two hundred mortgage banks went out of business.

Doubtless, it had been a great run. From 2000 to 2006, U.S. median home prices rose about 50 percent to an average $221,900. Whatever Americans were losing to inflation and stagnant wages during those boom years for housing, they were more than making up in their home values. Family income inched up only 14 percent during that period.

Yet home prices could outpace family income for only so long. After a while, the aberration had to disappear by what economists call "regressing to the mean," or returning to a historical average return, which is less than the rate of inflation when you subtract the myriad expenses of homeownership. In 1997, home prices were fairly close to their historical averages. Something happened three years later and home prices appreciated at rates no one had ever seen before.

## Bubble Profits Lost

Millions of homeowners who thought that their run at the housing craps table would continue unabated faced foreclosure or were forced into "short" sales for less than the mortgaged value. Their reasoning during the boom was simple and coldly rational: "If appreciation continues, I'll take out the lowest-cost loan with the least amount of money down." After all, wasn't homeownership built on the foundation of leverage?

Wall Street and the banking industry responded frenetically to this prevailing wisdom by passing along the risk of owning mortgages. Who was taking the risk on an interest-only loan? Certainly not the mortgage broker or bank, which got paid a fee if the mortgage closed and they resold the loan, which was "securitized" by a Wall Street banker. Clever financial engineers then packaged the mortgage with other securities in opaque vehicles called "tranches," or collateralized mortgage obligations. If interest rates went up in these adjustable-rate loans, the mortgage holder would just refinance or sell the house, it was assumed. And certainly ratings agencies that deemed these mortgage bundles to be of the highest quality weren't going to get hurt. They were only rating credit quality, not guaranteeing it.

As interest rates rose in late 2007 and the riskiest adjustable loans reset—making them unaffordable—foreclosures skyrocketed to an all-time high. The banking industry suddenly became Puritanical and effectively shut down the subprime and "Alt-A" markets for the highest-credit-risk borrowers. Even if those people wanted to refinance, their credit scores and incomes were so low that they didn't qualify for another loan. Many of them "piggybacked" other loans on top of their mortgage. Not that it mattered.

Nearly one-third of the adjustable loans didn't involve much of a down payment; almost half taking out loans in 2005 through 2006 put down nothing at all. The median down payment was 2 percent. Since those buyers had no skin in the game, they viewed their venture as pure speculation. If things didn't work out, they'd mail the keys to the bank and walk away. By early 2007, that's what was happening in neighborhoods from Florida to California.

Did no one along the way suspect this would be a problem? About 40 percent of all foreclosures were to those homeowners who couldn't make payments *before* their resets. What were the bankers thinking? The Federal Reserve and a bevy of banking regulators were hearing of the abuses but did nothing to stem them.

During the boom, homeowners made decisions that could be deemed rational. They pulled money out of their homes—nearly $600 billion in 2004 and 2005 alone. Most used the money to pay down other debts or improve their homes, but a frightening number used the equity to buy boats or cars or pay for vacations or college. Why not borrow against your home if it's appreciating at a double-digit rate? They thought that appreciation alone would rebuild their nest egg without them having to lift a muscle.

So much money was yanked from nest eggs by 2008 that Americans collectively owed more than they owned in their homes. Compare that to the typical post–World War II ethic of never touching home equity until retirement. In those days, homeowners stored up to 80 percent of their home equity. The irony of the "leverage as much as you can" ideology is that although homeowners saw this equity as free money, they had to borrow to get at it, plunging ever deeper into debt.

## Costs of the Crash

The fallout on leveraging one's castle to the hilt is that it convinced Americans that they didn't need to save outside of their homes. The U.S. savings rate turned negative during the bubble years. If your home is appreciating 20 percent a year, why fool around with savings bonds, CDs, or stocks? But seeing their home values tank was not the kind of crash most Americans expected. The shock reminded them that they didn't really have the money to spend. In early 2009, consumer confidence dropped to levels not seen since the dour days of Richard Nixon.

The pain was felt everywhere. Every taxing body dependent on home values was hurting. In California, the epicenter of the bust, where homeowners moved mountains to be able to afford a $600,000 starter home in or near the big cities, the state faced a $42 billion budget deficit. As the state with the highest number of foreclosures, the Golden State's government said it was going to see a decline of $25 billion in personal income and more than $600 billion in property values in 2008. Foreclosed homes fell off tax rolls. The lost revenue depleted coffers in Sacramento. Public agencies like police and fire departments cut their budgets. State legislatures from New York to California were forecasting budget shortfalls of more than $140 billion by mid-2010.

As homeowners left their homes and dumped them on a market that had a more than one-year supply of houses and condos, it created foreclosure gulches of unsold and abandoned houses that may take a decade to restore. Although a complete tally was unavailable, the Census Bureau estimated that more than 14 million homes were vacant in 2008. Some vacant homes became crack houses, further depressing neighborhood home values as they deteriorated. That created an economic death spiral that made it even more difficult to sell homes and maintain prices. Who wants to buy in a neighborhood where people can't afford their homes, prices are falling, and people are leaving in droves?

Even harder hit were areas where speculators ran amuck. So-called "flipper heavens" along the Florida coast and in Las Vegas, Phoenix, and retirement meccas saw price declines of 50 percent or more. Since they were overbuilt to begin with, those areas may not see a normal market return for years.

The expansionist logic of simply building where land was cheapest fomented a disaster as the sheer distance of homeowners from their workplaces financially hobbled those who had no access to public transportation. From California's central valleys to Long Island, home buyers moved anywhere they could to get a seemingly affordable price. With adjustable-rate loans as low as 4 percent (and in many cases no down payment required), buyers had a deceptively easy entrée into the home of their dreams. No commute was too far for them. Even two hundred miles a day was acceptable for some.

By the time the price of gas soared past $4 a gallon and the price of crude oil passed $140 a barrel in the summer of 2008, the killer commute had become *de rigueur* in the quest for one's castle. Sprawling urban areas with no public transit or connection to a central city, or "spurbs," will become ghost towns if high energy prices return and persist (both highly likely in a healthy economy). On top of the crushing expense of a long car commute, the trip is unhealthy and bad for the environment. Communities can't possibly thrive if their residents are constantly on the road. They become little more than transient rental locations. "These were bets on location, location, location— premised on the idea that people would be willing to live hours from anywhere for a chance to own a single-family home they could actually afford," noted editorial writer Holman Jenkins Jr. in the *Wall Street Journal*. "No federally sponsored haircut can put these housing bets back in the money or stop these houses from coming back on the market at distress prices."

The biggest losers have been those whose homes were foreclosed upon, facing a collective loss exceeding $164 billion. One out of five mortgages during the tail end of the bubble was subprime. The government's modest help for those homeowners provided some relief, yet those homes may still come back on the market at huge discounts. Free-market economists argue that this will eventually revive the housing market, but not before the creative destruction of capitalism has dislocated millions.

The U.S. and world economy also comes out on the short end. When homeowners don't feel pulse-racing gratification from their home appreciation—the so-called "wealth effect"—they stop spending in the general economy. For every dollar Americans lose in home values, they cut spending up to seven cents, according to Frederic Mishkin, a former Federal Reserve System governor. That's roughly $155 billion that's sucked out of consumer spending, far overshadowing the pathetic economic rebate stimulus package Congress passed in February 2007, when home foreclosures were effectively doubling compared to the previous year.

## A Cultural Obsession

The profound economic loss of a housing bust trickles down through the economy like water from a leaky roof that slowly destroys the interior of a home. Many Americans who had set a date for retirement will be working longer—particularly if they were planning on selling their homes and downsizing to more-affordable quarters. The stock-market bust that started in 2008 compounded the misery. Even before the housing bubble burst, stocks eroded retirement wealth. The Standard & Poor's 500 Index lost almost 50 percent between September 2001 and September 2002. To make matters worse, many investors, losing faith in their 401(k) plans, curtailed their saving and plunged into the housing market, figuring that stocks were unsafe, but homes weren't.

Stung by stock-market losses from the dot-com bust, ordinary home-owners got so caught up in the housing frenzy that they believed they could start over as real estate investors. Investment homes would become not only their retirement fund but also their college savings kitty! Castles of any size could be profitable as long as land became scarcer. After all, they weren't making any more of it, and this was the height of George W. Bush's "ownership society." Besides, wasn't it a staple of the American project that one could emerge from any financial or cultural backwa-ter and reinvent oneself as an entrepreneur? Nobody really believed F. Scott Fitzgerald when he said (in essence) there "are no second acts in American life."

To observe the deeper implications of these questions, we need to go to a place where the American dream walked hand in hand with enter-tainment, optimism, sunshine, and unbridled speculation: Florida.

# PART 1

A Dream
Gone Bad

# CHAPTER 1

# False Economics
## American Dreamers
## in the Sunshine State

IT IS ALL OF seven degrees and snow is dancing around me like devilish ice pixies as I assemble the bike rack for our family van. On my back on the frozen driveway with a socket wrench, I'm wearing four layers under my arctic parka. It's not shaping up to be a warm February. Nothing is thawing. It's just getting colder. So much for global warming this year. Chicago winters have a habit of lingering like unwanted guests; they chill you to the corpuscle, often well into May. I couldn't have picked a better month to leave Chicago for Florida.

We're heading for a rental home in Bonita Springs, a relatively small patch of beach and inland area nestled between Naples and Fort Myers on the southwest coast. I wanted to not only experience the housing boom first hand by staying in what was then one of the hottest areas on the continent but also gain an understanding of how investors were faring as the housing market ebbed.

The sunshine is ample as we enter Florida, and the promotional signs begin popping up for theme parks, orange stands, and other amusements. This is the visceral America, a region where everything is for sale all of the time. Few limits are set on the amount of land that can be purchased for the all-consuming, nor are there any guidelines on how to restrain the unquenchable thirst for soil, water, air, and minerals. Florida is what we've been and what we've become: Churches and gated communities. History and amnesia. Vitality and death. God's waiting room. The promised land. Disney this, Universal that. The alpha and omega. The whole Hegelian banana. For baby boomers, it's the place we may loathe and the place where we might end up, a parental state that nurtures with its abundant warmth and scorns with its violent tropical temperament. Graced with water and solar energy, it's the land of plenty that's being depleted daily as more than one thousand people a day trundle in during the good times, hoping for a better life.

Theme park marketing captivated the American home buyer during the housing boom. New American homes and the cul-de-sac pods that incubated them became a *destination*. Why go to a bank to see a grandiose marble floor when it could be in your very own bathroom or grand entrance? Names conveyed images of pleasure and elite comfort, even though the developments' names had nothing to do with the places they were named after. Your hacienda would be waiting for you in the Spanish Wells development. Refined elegance could be enjoyed at the Monte Carlo or Wyndemere. Want to commune with the spirit of nature? Cypress Preserve or Cedar Hammock offered a unique experience. Never mind that the original settlers and abundant wetlands were long gone.

In cul-de-sac heaven, foyers were transformed from mere vestibules to grand portals of paradise. Private spaces became statements of pure ego and the subjugation of nature. Why venture out in the wilderness to see a waterfall or hot springs when it could be produced in your very own shower or bathtub?

Upgrading one's lifestyle in the housing boom meant producing a spectacle, something that would entertain you and your friends without your needing to leave home. Kitchens featured commercial-quality stoves and refrigerators. Yet these appliances didn't ensure that people would be cooking or eating in any more than they used to—owners wanted to project the appearance that their home was a *must-see*. This was the superficial aspect of the housing boom that hadn't changed much since the days of the robber barons. Daniel McGinn called this predilection "house lust" (he authored a book of the same name), a nearly loony infatuation with the image homeowners hoped to create. Marble, granite, and huge amounts of unusable space conveyed a Palladian sensibility in a suburban locale.

What became more important to Americans than the appearance of a dwelling was a drive to build wealth the easy way—through residential housing. After all, did a house depreciate significantly during one's lifetime? The little slumps in Los Angeles and Boston in the late 1980s and early 1990s were long forgotten when the home market started its ascent in 2001. A whole generation of GIs and their families built homes with generous government assistance after World War II and were rewarded with enormous nest eggs. Was there any reason to believe that home appreciation *wasn't* guaranteed in the twenty-first century? The doctrine of the infallibility of the home as an investment attracted perhaps more true believers in Florida than in any other state, morphing into a speculators' bacchanal in a few, brief years.

## The Home as an Investment

Beth and Fabrizio (Fab) Faieta knew the ebb and flow of quirky real estate markets. Born and raised in the Boston area, they learned that to make money on property, you had to sit on it for years and be patient. They weren't out to make a quick profit by "flipping" a home after owning it for only a few months. They were *investors*. They were trying to do the right thing by making money on real estate long term and pursuing a better life in the Sunshine State. They weren't getting ahead by investing in their retirement plans. Massachusetts taxes ate up their incomes. They believed so much in the prospect of real estate that they cashed out both of their retirement plans when they were in their forties. All they had left was about $2,000 in an individual retirement account. They were entrepreneurs in the purest sense, striving for some measure of financial independence.

Arriving from the Boston area in 2004, they started investing in Florida homes as a way to create a nest egg and accumulate college savings for their two young daughters. Beth is attractive and talented, once a professional Shania Twain impressionist. Her business is selling hair extensions. Fab is a beefy, garrulous building tradesman. Both are devoted Red Sox fans. The Faietas were sold on Florida real estate after one of Fab's friends showed up on their doorstep and extolled the virtues of the Naples area. So the balmy weather sealed the deal, and Fab went into business with him. As owners of three investment properties in the Boston area, the Faietas picked up in Florida where they left off in New England. They had been landlords since they met nearly a decade ago, so they were acquainted with the expenses and difficulties of rental ownership. They had also made good profits on the homes they sold. "We came to Florida to have a bit of an easier life without snow, I guess," Beth told me. "And we invested here just as we did up north. We knew how to fix up homes and be excellent landlords."

When I did my Florida research, I stayed in one of the five homes they had bought. A three-bedroom ranch with a two-car garage, it was fairly typical of entry-level homes in Florida. At the time I rented the house, it was listed for $395,000. At first, the price seemed inflated, but this was Florida at the end of the boom. Some one-third of properties in southwest Florida were bought by speculators at the height of the mania. Ordinary homes like these were overpriced and swamped a market already swimming in countless unsold properties when I was touring the state. The Bonita home, though, was bought at a relative bargain. The Faietas paid $260,000 for it in September 2004, which was fairly close to the average at the time for that kind of home in Florida.

When low interest rates unleashed a wave of rampant speculation throughout the country, the Faietas were aggressive in grabbing cheap financing. They landed a mortgage for the Bonita home at 4.62 percent, a rate not seen in a generation. Thanks to a Federal Reserve captained by "Maestro" Alan Greenspan, it was hoped that a deep recession could be averted after the stock market crash of 2000 and the tragedy of September 11, 2001. What happened to home prices could have been anticipated, yet the prospect was somehow ignored as middle-class Americans feasted on the cornucopia of low mortgage rates and the numerous property-related tax breaks.

Following the freewheeling *zeitgeist,* the Faietas were quick to realize that real estate could be their ticket to accumulate wealth in a short period of time. They had no reason to believe otherwise. They weren't going to make money in the stock market or investing in savings bonds. From 2001 through 2005, large-company stocks returned a miserable 0.54 percent. When you subtracted the inflation of 2.5 percent during that period, big stocks weren't even worth the postage needed to open a brokerage account. Ultrasafe U.S. Treasury bills weren't much better, yielding only about 2 percent during that time. The dot-com/day-trading days were ancient history. Although stocks that invested in small companies and commercial real estate were doing well during the large-company swoon, most individual investors either eschewed them—seeing them as another huge stock market risk—or simply didn't know about them. So when the housing market went into overdrive, millions who had been pining over their devastated 401(k)s were ready for action. "We purchased the Bonita house—and the others—thinking that we would like to keep them long term," Beth said when I first asked why she and Fab invested in Florida real estate. "We're not flippers."

## Climbing Ownership Costs During the Boom

As the Faietas discovered, buying and holding real estate isn't like owning a stock. You can't always control ownership expenses. When a wave of hurricanes blew across Florida in 2005, an aftershock of insurance premium increases hit the Sunshine State. The premium for the Bonita home went from a reasonable $999 a year to $1,407. For another home the Faietas owned in nearby Naples, the cost soared from $2,400 to $7,400. The insurance premiums were compounded by rising property prices, which meant higher assessed values—resulting in skyrocketing property-tax hikes.

When the Faietas bought the Bonita home, the annual tax bill was a bargain at $1,200. By the end of 2006, it had climbed to $3,768. Property taxes weren't just rising in southwest Florida. Every home with higher values was subject to a higher real estate taxes. Unless there is an assessment cap (as in places like California), assessors are free to track home markets.

The unintended consequence of the housing bubble was that it caused property-tax rates to soar by double digits in many places, making home ownership even more unaffordable. Newer homes in freshly developed areas usually got hit the hardest. Americans then got stung by a "sprawl" tax, which was perfectly legal yet never voted on nor anticipated. Spurbs where building was heaviest and home values the highest saw the greatest increases. Within three years, homes that once were bargains became financial burdens unless they were sold off. Those who thought they were getting the deal of a lifetime courtesy of low mortgage rates got caught in the cul-de-sac syndrome: They borrowed more than they could really afford, moved farther out from central cities, and gambled on home appreciation. Developers, elected officials, bankers, and Wall Street suffered from the same malady. They too refused to believe that these investments would ever sour. Although this thinking had been prevalent for generations, it escalated into a mass hysteria during the boom years.

By early 2007, blindsided by soaring ownership costs, the Faietas had slashed the prices on their homes. They cut the Bonita home's listing price by $50,000. There were no takers as more than ten thousand properties glutted the southwest Florida market. Although they had previously been able to sell on their own, this time the Faietas hired a real estate agent, whose commission would cut into their profits. The boom days were a distant memory, a sharp contrast to 2004, when, the Faietas recalled, "we had to put in offers on the same day or the home was gone."

As I prepared to leave the Faietas' Bonita home, local real estate broker Douglas Brunner told me he was selling homes at 20 to 33 percent discounts. A year later, when I checked in with Beth, the Faietas still hadn't sold their homes and were borrowing heavily on their credit cards to keep their heads above water. The Bonita home's listing price was now $279,900, but they were still able to rent it out. Taxes on the home had eased somewhat, to $3,000, but the Faietas owed $12,500 in taxes for a lot and home in Naples and a duplex in Cape Coral. Taxes on their own home soared to $7,600. Insurance premiums had dropped, though their total bill was almost $8,000 for all of their properties. A new Florida property-tax law offered them little relief.

"It seems I can't stop talking about our troubles with our home," Beth wrote me in early 2008, adding that their real estate woes had put intense pressure on their marriage. They fought constantly over what to do. "It's very stressful for us to be in the position we're in. We haven't sold anything and I fear our credit score will soon be going south. People aren't into the 'little upgrade brings more value' idea right now. It's a shame they don't see the big picture. We don't even have the Naples home listed with a realtor right now because they need a guarantee that they would make their commission at the short sale price [selling it for less than the mortgaged value]. I've listed it on Zillow and Craigslist for $399,900. But we owe more than that on it."

The Faietas' housing woes didn't stop with those two homes. A duplex they owned in Cape Coral, where they live, was fully rented, although netting $600 less than their expenses for the unit. "The problem is, we bought it in the summer of '06 when things were priced at their highest, so we can't refinance that one," Beth said. Like many who availed themselves of low rates when they became available, the Faietas had multiple mortgages on their properties. On their duplex, they had one 8.25 percent loan and another at 13 percent. They spent $25,000 remodeling the duplex, and it was worth $50,000 less than what they owed. The saving grace was that the house they lived in was financed with an 8.25 percent fixed-rate mortgage. Expenses on all five properties tripled in the time they have owned them, and by 2008 they could barely afford to pay half of their mortgages.

"We have always tried to invest for our kids' futures. We have never tried to flip. We actually liked being landlords. We are doing better this year than last with our businesses, but every cent is going to toward our bills. I'm really tired of it and have decided to stop paying a few and stop stressing out. It's just hard to decide which ones. Once we sell a few of them [houses], we're going to bank our money for a while until we can buy the home we want to live in permanently and then think about our next step. I only hope we don't ruin the excellent credit we used to have. Some days there is $32 in our account, and some days enough to pay most of our bills, but we're making sure we can afford groceries and gas first."

## Spurb Corridors

The Faietas' home and investment properties became mired in a foreclosure alley that ran from Tampa to Dade County. Cape Coral was among the top-twenty markets for numbers of defaults. Places where previously there had been relatively little development turned into boomtowns because homeowners—and later speculators—snatched up properties with cheap mortgage money. Places like Lehigh Acres, just southeast of Cape Coral, became clusters of condos and single-family homes. They weren't the traditional suburbs of larger regional cities like Fort Myers or Naples. Their only connection was the knotted, constantly expanding Route 41 and I-75, which run from Tampa to Fort Myers and Miami.

Most of the newer communities that were ravaged by the housing bust had almost no central core, little in terms of local or regional master planning, no mass transportation, and few established services or infrastructure. As spurbs, they were the mushrooms of unsustainable sprawl. And they weren't confined to Florida.

In the vast California interior, which is mostly desert or mountains, you find Lancaster, incorporated in 1977, or Hesperia, established in 1988. Both originally were refuges for buyers seeking affordable homes in the greater Los Angeles area. But these arid towns were nowhere near the city. Hesperia is ninety miles away from the city of angels. Residents settling in many cities that sprung up east and south of San Francisco and Silicon Valley faced several hours of commuting—one way. By 2008, they were subprime gulches, as those homeowners defaulted on adjustable loans that put them one rate increase away from unaffordability.

Nevada led the other states in home defaults. Miami's prices fell more than 37 percent from 2005 to 2008. Prices in some areas in California dropped more than 35 percent, and countless homeowners have sent their keys back to the bank ("jingle mail") and walked away in the middle of the night.

## To the Manor Bought

Why was the American psyche so heavily invested in homeownership? The need to start anew and reinvent was one of the undeniable messages of the building boom. We constructed new palaces of consumption because it was in our American DNA. Each new home became a mini theme park. The McMansions so often ridiculed by aesthetes embody this need to convey wealth, status, and tradition—the same need that made owners try to make their homes look like French chateaus, English country homes, or Gothic castles.

The American home became the embodiment of generations of aspirations. First came the land, then came the emblem that you owned and lorded over the landscape—the manor home. In a uniquely American way, homeowners were echoing the class-climbing impulses of their forebears. Cathedral ceilings bespoke of sanctified self-improvement. Bathroom suites implied middle-class barony. Homes got bigger and more expensive because we wanted them to portray nobility. We had made it. We'd achieved the American dream! This was what we had to show for generations of effort. The fact that this striving also became a mania for investment and speculation is also painfully American.

The lure of riches and adventure has been the transformative American quest ever since European monarchs cast their eyes on North America beginning in the late fifteenth century and financed adventurers like Sir Walter Raleigh to start colonies. What originally was a search for a shorter route to India and China also was a search for El Dorado, the city of gold. Even young Samuel Clemens was smitten by the gold bug when he ventured west in the middle of the nineteenth century. Whether they came from moribund little towns, shtetls, farms, or impoverished mining communities, they had a need to reinvent themselves, becoming the future gentry.

Sudden wealth grants the power to reinvent one's persona. Overnight, we hurdle from the bowels of the lower or middle class into a higher echelon of society. Just like the unsinkable Molly Brown, whose husband accidentally discovers a vein of gold on his Colorado homestead, we propel ourselves into another world. The home becomes the symbol of our newly acquired privileges and worldly goods. The mansion buys our prestige and status in a world where those attainments contribute immeasurably to self-worth.

Even a humble trailer home or two-bedroom condo is a sanctified place in American culture. It's a shrine to our independence and accomplishment, a symbol that we've thrown off the yoke of our indentured servitude. Investing in homes took that process one step further as the holy grail became financial independence. Homes were no longer castles, in the cul-de-sac era. They were receptacles and generators of wealth. For the Faietas, they were entrepreneurial retirement plans in a world in which 401(k) plans were for suckers. There was nothing wrong with the concept of building wealth through land, of course. It had been ingrained in our cultural DNA for four hundred years.

Like the conquistadors, cul-de-sac prospectors favored warm places and flocked to Phoenix, Las Vegas, Miami, and southwest Florida during the housing bubble days. If you believed in the dream—and leveraged to the hilt to get there—you too could be free from future financial worry. It was all part of the same fantasy.

Wall Street and the banks wanted us to realize our dream and enabled it in every way possible—even if we couldn't afford the mortgages to buy these vestiges of acquired status. Government also did its part: It had been pushing home and property ownership since Europeans first began to settle on the continent and usurped the land from the natives. America was built on the premise that people like the Faietas could succeed and prosper. Millions did.

Where did this overpowering obsession for a completely new life and dwelling come from? How did land and house become entwined with our ideas of a Gibraltar-like investment? To answer those questions, I traveled to tidewater Virginia, where the origins of the American dream were firmly rooted.

# CHAPTER 2

# Origins of a Dream

I AM AT the crest of Monticello, standing on the grassy front porch of Thomas Jefferson's home, one of the most famous in the world. The sky is radiant, and I try to imagine what he saw when he gazed westward and envisioned the future. It's not likely that he envisioned the gated, mock-Mediterranean Floridian villas shackled to golf courses or the endless tract-home ghettos of centerless suburbia. I doubt that he would have been sanguine about the cul-de-sac society unless it involved working farms and a modicum of self-sufficiency.

To understand the American preoccupation with property, I decide to literally walk in Jefferson's footsteps. Transported back in time, I picture myself as the young, lanky red-haired student, always peeking around an intellectual corner in Williamsburg, Virginia. Jefferson arrived here at age seventeen in 1760 and was educated at the College of William and Mary, obtaining his legal training there. Possessing a strong build, firm jaw, and insatiable mind, he was educating himself in the capital of England's crown colony, jewel of the Hanoverian kings, nexus for the mid-Atlantic tobacco industry, and one of the wealthiest North American enclaves outside of Philadelphia and Boston. This was the young man's intellectual base camp, the firmament for someone who would have more influence in shaping the real estate of the continent than any other man of his time.

Jefferson would peer down the generously wide main street of this colonial utopia, laid out at exactly ninety-nine feet wide by Governor Francis Nicholson, who wanted a gracious green space lined with trees in the middle of his boulevard, an elegant template for thousands of towns yet to be born. The designer of Annapolis, Maryland, Nicholson

Thomas Jefferson's Monticello, looking west
*Credit:* Thomas Jefferson Foundation

also sought to emulate an Edinburgh-like "royal mile" with his Duke of Gloucester Street, an axis that boasted of the College of William and Mary on one end and the Capitol Building on the other. In between were the Bruton Parish Church, a courthouse and public commons, taverns, carriage makers, blacksmiths, wigmakers, an apothecary, and a smattering of smaller private residences. Jefferson couldn't help admiring the symmetry of the town, with the governor's palace on the leg of a T-shaped design.

As a white, male, Protestant landowner, Jefferson would serve in Virginia's House of Burgesses, one of the incubators of the American Revolution, which was scarcely a mile from the governor's palace, a building Jefferson would later briefly occupy as revolutionary governor of Virginia. It's hard to know exactly what moved Jefferson's soul in those days or what the town looked like before John D. Rockefeller Jr. reconstructed it. For young Jefferson, Williamsburg was likely akin to Puritan leader John Winthrop's "city upon a hill," at least in terms of a place of privilege for a white member of the landed class.

But was Jefferson tortured by the forced labor provided by slaves, a practice he *hoped* would be abolished? Although slavery as an economic institution was brutal and unsustainable, there was little Jefferson did personally to change the status quo in his own life at Monticello, even though the "pursuit of happiness" ideally extended to everyone. This noble ideal amended John Locke's 1689 dictum that "the great and chief end, therefore, of Mens uniting into Commonwealths, and putting themselves under Government, is the Preservation of their *Property* [italics mine]." And property entitled some people to certain unalienable rights in *that* world.

"The Founding Generation believed that property supported security, independence and autonomy," writes historian Calvin Jillson in *Pursuing the American Dream*, "but Jefferson's 'pursuit of happiness' suggests a goal well beyond security that we might call human fulfillment and thriving."

## Jefferson's Broader Vision

When the Revolutionary War ended and Jefferson returned from France, he saw a country being quilted into a vast, unfolding neatly laid out network of farms and towns connected by commerce and anchored by democracy. Monticello and Charlottesville were the epicenter of the creation of this brave, man-made new world. Despite his noble words in the Declaration of Independence, Jefferson sought to expand a broad concept that could not be sustained. Even the principal author of the Declaration was not willing to free more than a handful of his slaves.

An obsessive long-term remodeler, Jefferson was constantly building, rebuilding, and tearing down his domicile. From 1796 to 1809, Monticello must have looked like a wreck. Nevertheless, Jefferson not only created a triumph of agricultural promise with his ornamental farm on a mountain, he also laid out a plan of what he saw for the rest of the continent. From his perch, he imagined the gridiron of towns and farms that was the foundation of the 1784 land ordinance, in the creation of which he was actively involved.

"In part," writes Jefferson scholar William Beiswanger, "the grid can be explained by the country's interest in quickly settling a vast, unexplored part of the continent. But Jefferson's preference for this form is evident again in a proposal made while president in 1805 for 'chequer-board' towns with buildings constructed on the black squares and white ones 'left open in turf and trees.' Every house would front an open square, and the atmosphere of such a town would be like that of the country." Sound familiar?

Jefferson was not only synthesizing his youthful impression of Williamsburg but also thinking beyond it to small towns and the suburbs. America would expand far beyond his beloved Blue Ridge Mountains. It would be an enlightened development led by yeoman farmers. The key to this master plan: a massive acquisition and settlement of discrete parcels of land into subdivisions. It was precise. Eventually it would become a bulwark of democracy.

He likely imagined precisely organized towns and townships within the lines of his grid, a blueprint that goes back all the way to the formation of the Greek city of Piraeus in 450 B.C. One of the big "checkerboard" cities of Jefferson's time was Philadelphia, based on the model of Sir Christopher Wren's new plan for London, which had been devastated by fire in 1666. The city of brotherly love planned its grid in 1682, followed by Savannah in 1733 and New York City in 1811. The radial streets of Washington, DC, were envisioned by Pierre-Charles L'Enfant in 1791.

What did Jefferson foresee as he exulted at the top of his little mountain? Was it the idyllic intercontinental quilt of farms run by white, Protestant gentlemen like him? Was it, as architect William McDonough surmises, "the orderly grid of the enlightenment"? Would the final product look like the steroidal waffle iron of Levittown or the graceful curves of Riverside, Illinois? Could order even be imposed on an unruly continent now forever dedicated to commerce, endless expansion, and the dream of a homestead for every family?

## Land Deal of the Century

Whatever blueprints Jefferson had in his magnificent mind, the continent would be forever imprinted by his vision. Jefferson's plan for the burgeoning Anglo-American population made him an *ecodynamo,* someone who could spur change in entire systems. The third president was vaguely aware of the potential of the land west of the Mississippi River, seeking to expand trade routes to the then-mythical water route to the Pacific (John Smith of Jamestown fame was also looking for this passage).

With the Louisiana Purchase—bought for about 3 cents an acre in 1803—Jefferson transacted one of the most astounding real estate deals in history and negated Napoleon Bonaparte's agreement with the Spanish to cede the territory to France. Strategically, the purchase allowed the growing American republic to control the Mississippi basin, a vital artery for trade and commerce. Keeping the river out of European hands was essential.

The audacious way the French acquired the land in the first place was one of many arrogant moves of European imperialism, one that would set a precedent for centuries. The great French explorer René-Robert Cavelier, sieur de La Salle, discovered a way from Montreal to the mouth of the Mississippi through the Great Lakes and Indian canoe routes. When he reached the point where the Big Muddy emptied into the Gulf of Mexico in 1682, he claimed the entire river's drainage area—more than 1 million square miles—for King Louis XIV.

Jefferson saw great trade and commercial opportunities springing from the great river's basin. Like many surreptitious European land grabs, Louisiana became the subject of scandal when Scottish financier John Law tried to sell shares in a French colony fronted by the Mississippi Company in the early eighteenth century. By inflating the value and potential of Louisiana, Law marketed stock to thousands who speculated in shares of his company, creating the continent's first stock and real estate bubble. The scheme collapsed in 1720, forcing Law to flee France, leaving impoverished investors in his wake and sowing the seeds for the French Revolution.

The strategy of claiming massive swaths of land worked well for the Europeans because the natives had no concept of trusts, deeds, or titles. During the colonization of Massachusetts, author Nathaniel Philbrick notes, "Instead of a title and deed, the Indians' relationship to the land was based on a complex mixture of cultural factors, with the sachem (chief) possessing a right to distribute land in his own territory."

The natives, often composed of loose confederations of nomadic tribes, were not town builders who laid out formal squares, meeting halls, and churches. Native Americans didn't see land as an economic asset; it was a gift over which they had stewardship. They didn't need property for the purpose of "enriching themselves," as the Plymouth colony Governor William Bradford claimed disdainfully. As American history unfolded, New England would be ravaged by a series of wars against the natives, a genocidal cultural clash that would continue through the end of the nineteenth century. Land became the object of individual possession, as property-starved peasants, yeomen, and religious emigrants poured in from Europe seeking to start a new life with a simple piece of land to farm.

At the time of the Louisiana sale, Napoleon needed the money to continue his warring and had lost interest in the New World. Alarmed by the closing of the port of New Orleans in 1802, Jefferson not only wanted to secure trade on the Mississippi and limit British and Spanish interests, he needed to extend commerce deep into the land's unknown interior and open up a new route untrammeled by the British to the Pacific. Jefferson envisioned a water transportation system that would connect the Mississippi to the Great Lakes—linked by the navigable Illinois to the "portage of only two miles to the Chickago [Chicago], which affords a batteau navigation of 16 miles to its entrance into Lake Michigan." The fur trade also loomed large.

Leverage was the key to doubling the size of the country. Jefferson put his young nation $13 million into debt over the next fifteen years, although he believed that commercial growth and new taxes would pay for the acquisition. In his third annual message to Congress, he noted, "The ordinary annual augmentation of imposts from increasing population and wealth . . . and the economies which still may be introduced into our public expenditures" would pay the debt service.

The epitome of the Virginia planter—an identity he could never escape—Jefferson saw land begetting cash crops. People settling on the land would eventually pay taxes to cover the purchase of more land. The perspective he adopted was that land was a cheaply valued asset that would eventually produce income, although he understood little what the commodification of this land—and the extirpation of the Native Americans living there—would ultimately cost his fledgling republic.

In the autumn of his life, though hopelessly mired in debt, Jefferson was in his native element on his sacred mountain. I suspect that when he looked west, he envisioned an America much like what he had attempted to create at Monticello: Large estates with independent farmers would dot the land in the townships he imagined in the Ordinance of 1784. These farms would have their own cottage industries producing everything from beer to furniture, even making their own nails. He must have reasoned that technology would save the country from "the peculiar institution" of slavery at some future point.

Visions aside, by the time Jefferson finished work on his last masterpiece—the "academical village" of the University of Virginia—

nearly all of burgeoning America would bear his stamp, both philosophically and physically.

## Sacred Places: Homes as Moral Bastions

The age of Jeffersonian reason held sway in the form of the grid in most suburban developments with only a few exceptions. Within a generation of Jefferson's death, Llewellyn Park in West Orange, New Jersey, was one of the first planned communities in America to break the grid, in 1857. Shortly after the Civil War, in 1868, Frederick Law Olmsted and Calvert Vaux planned Riverside, Illinois. Built near a fairly undesirable piece of property about eleven miles from Chicago, Riverside was the antigrid community. When I drive through Riverside, I immediately sense that the legendary landscape designers wanted a more natural environment that would provide a salve for people wanting to escape the horrors of a nineteenth-century city.

Through the middle of the community, along the Des Plaines River and in view of every home, is green space. Long "commons" provide a serpentine strip of greenery that runs like a natural buffer through the heart of Riverside. William Le Baron Jenney, one of the fathers of the skyscraper, built his home there as well as a medieval-looking water tower in the form of a turret. Olmsted and Vaux designed every detail of the community, from the water works to seven hundred acres of public space. It was hardly Jefferson's scheme of yeoman farmers on square plots, but it extended the privileges of open land to all residents, an even more democratic notion of land use that would rarely be repeated in future communities.

To Olmsted and Vaux, who would design hundreds of parks and towns throughout the country, the *land* was sacred. It needed to be preserved and nurtured for the betterment and health of its inhabitants. Land was not a commodity to them. It was under the purview of the soul. Like the home, it was a sacred place.

Homes were sanctified spaces as well. The origin of the home as the sacred vessel of domesticity has deep roots that go back thousands of years. The cruciform design of many seminal American homes and communities is deeply influenced by the sacred architecture found in churches and cathedrals. As secular America rose from the promises of the Revolution and the Enlightenment, the subtle connection to sacred elements became more subdued. To this day, trophy homes and mock-medieval McMansions have cathedral ceilings and stained-glass and leaded windows. The pointed arch itself may have come from Islamic architecture via the Crusaders. Whatever its origin, the aesthetic sense of the Gothic style never left the cultural legacy of homebuilding. Spurred by the great artist and architectural critic John Ruskin, the Gothic Revival in the mid–nineteenth century was a profound influence on homebuilders throughout the United States. For Ruskin, the Gothic symbolized "the confession of imperfection and the desire of change." The growing but unsteady American republic embodied both of those ideas and added one more guideline that would be captured in homebuilding: moral character. Catharine Beecher, sister of Harriet Beecher Stowe, the world-famous author of *Uncle Tom's Cabin,* and daughter of the famous preacher Lyman, laid the groundwork for how an American home should look and run. Her *Treatise on Domestic Economy* in 1841, at the height of the Transcendentalism period, dictated that "there is no matter of domestic economy which more seriously involves the health and daily comfort of American women than the proper construction of houses."

The oldest of nine, Catharine later teamed up with her sister Harriet after their mother died to produce another influential book on home-making. Flush with royalties from her bestselling classic, Harriet built her Hartford dream house "Oakholm" in grand Gothic style in 1863. It reflected her ideals of a "comfortable, healthy Christian home," although it proved unlivable after a few years. Yet this was a house with a message of spirituality. The subtle arches built in the home and the hundreds of thousands that would be built afterward in other homes represented "the passion of faith," according to architectural historian Jonathan Hale. The predominant arch is based on a mandorla, or almond, which is an ancient symbol of life and wholeness, or the "materialization of the spirit." Several generations of Victorian homes in the Italianate, Second Empire, and Queen Anne styles would mimic this theme.

While the Beechers were mainly writing for women, landscape architect Andrew Jackson Downing wanted all of genteel America to rejoice in the rural spiritual revival of the Gothic style. "What an unfailing barrier against vice, immorality, and bad habits" was the Gothic home of his time, detailed in several floor plans in his influential 1856 edition of *Cottage Residences.* Not only could homes be stately and beautiful, they also could be strongholds of morality. The country home provided a moat against all of the evil, pollution, pestilence, and licentiousness of the city. It became a sanctuary at a time when cities were ravaged by cholera, tuberculosis, filthy air, and poisoned water. Motivated by "evangelical piety" and the picturesque, Downing and Beecher would set the tone for the nineteenth-century ex-urban home.

Throughout the rest of the nineteenth century, "Carpenter Gothic" style for the masses introduced miniature flying buttresses under roof eaves. Pointed arches highlighted dramatic windows. Stained glass was everywhere. When the neo-Gothic movement gave way to the Arts and Crafts Movement, which was inspired by Ruskin's writing in the latter half of the nineteenth century, the home became even more sacred in its decoration. Frank Lloyd Wright's early prairie-style homes basked in stained or leaded glass. The most modern home dwellings of the twentieth century still clung to the sacredness of the Gothic. Even powerhouse banker J. P. Morgan's Medici-class library on Murray Hill in New York invokes the deity through an inscription in stone as you walk in to gawk at three stories of ancient books—many of them bibles—collected from all over the world. Apparently, one of the world's most powerful capitalists thought it fit to praise the creator in his own castle. Although they became more abstract, stained and leaded glass treatments survived well into the twentieth century, with some of the most modern homes today incorporating designs that are thousands of years old.

## A Revolution in Building Technology and Design

The sacred symbolism of the neo-Gothic movement proceeded hand in hand with the revolution in building, finance, and other technologies. In Chicago during the 1830s, the balloon frame became the dominant form of home construction. Instead of using awkward, heavy post-and-beam framing, it employed two-by-four wooden studs in "stick-built" walls that could be assembled much more quickly and at a lower cost of labor and materials. This single construction method still dominates American homebuilding and is used in building 90 percent of all new homes.

The balloon frame was the core technology of American home building as the country moved west. The Homestead Act, signed by Abraham Lincoln in 1862, literally gave 160 acres to any adult male who was a citizen or intended to become one. That opened up 83 million acres to settlement initially. Some 15 million more were added in Colorado, California, and Washington. All a man had to do was stay on the land for five years and pay a small fee.

The Enlarged Homestead Act of 1909 offered even larger tracts—provided that the settler could furnish irrigation. Of course, many of the areas open to settlement would never support the kind of agriculture that thrived in the Eastern Plains and Upper Midwest. There simply wasn't enough rain. And once again, land lust and blanket claims on land given away by Washington forced the epic murder and relocation of Native Americans.

While homes were going up more quickly, cities became taller with the advance of steelmaking technology. When the skyscraper age began in Chicago in the early 1880s, barely a decade after most of the central city burned to the ground, suburban expansion became less of a sacred project and more of a utilitarian requirement for housing the huddling masses—many of whom were acquiring new wealth and had the means to escape the overcrowded cities. And flee they did, eventually using Henry Ford's new contraption, seen as a revolutionary, liberating force by Frank Lloyd Wright and other progressive thinkers of the time.

"The city is doomed and we shall solve the city problem by leaving the city," Ford declared. Ford was able to sell cars by the millions, but there was one glaring problem in the first decade of the twentieth century: Where would people go? The suburbs as we know them today largely didn't exist, and about 64 percent of Americans were renters. Only 12 percent owned property in New York; 18 percent in Boston.

Thanks to new tax breaks (passed in 1913) that allowed homeowners to deduct mortgage interest and property taxes from their income tax and a boom in building, homeownership took off in the 1920s. Rising wages after the recession of 1919 also fueled home buying. Between 1922 and 1927, nearly 1 million homes per year were built and nearly every city was suddenly ringed by new suburbs.

## Revolutionary Home Financing and the New Deal

The creation of the suburbs didn't follow a straight line in the early twentieth century. When the stock market crashed in 1929, homebuilding collapsed, and foreclosures soared during the Great Depression that followed. Franklin Delano Roosevelt aggressively sought to buoy homeownership by promoting the Home Owners' Loan Corporation (HOLC) in 1933. The new agency provided more than $3 billion for more than 1 million mortgages and prevented hundreds of thousands of foreclosures. The HOLC also introduced to the home market a major innovation: a long-term, self-amortizing mortgage. Now you could extend your debt for up to twenty years, which, in turn, allowed you to buy more house with a lower payment. It became the model for fixed-rate financing.

During the 1920s, mortgages were typically granted for five to ten years and put the homeowner at the mercy of the bond market when they came due. This financing made possible places like Radburn, New Jersey, in 1929, which pushed the boundaries of the metropolitan area into Olmsted-like expanses of homes and parks. "Security and happiness" was the theme of Radburn, based on Ebenezer Howard's design for garden cities.

The HOLC was followed by the Federal Housing Administration (FHA) and the Veterans Administration loan program in 1944. Neither program actually lent money; each simply guaranteed payment of mortgages for qualifying buyers. That ensured repayment for lenders and brought rates down. The FHA was a huge success in spurring homebuilding, and helped more than 11 million families buy their own homes. And the economics were appealing as well: For a $550 down payment you could buy a starter home and pay only about $30 a month over twenty years.

By lowering the cost of homeownership, the government was subsidizing financial independence. Renters became owners and established new communities, from the Craftsman bungalows of Los Angeles to Levittown, New York. Although many of these communities were almost exclusively white—with racist redlining promoted by FHA guidelines— they grew seemingly without limits or planning. Anchored by homeownership, Americans became the richest people on earth up until the 1970s, when the economy soured due to energy and inflation woes.

Growth was the powerful engine moving America into the future in the post-war era. The population increased by 12 million between 1945 and 1950 alone. My cohort, baby boomers, grew to 77 million strong. No generation has had such a consistent run of prosperity, educational opportunity, advances in health care, and affordable homeownership.

As America came unglued during the tumult of the Vietnam years, homeownership became the common goal that nearly every policymaker could agree on. Everyone emigrating from somewhere else or living in a tenement wanted his own home. As Jim Cullen recounts in *The American Dream*:

> Wherever they happened to live, Americans seemed united by an exceptional penchant for homeownership. It is notable, but perhaps not coincidental, that the greatest fervor appeared to come from immigrants. One study of Detroit, for example, showed that in 1900, 55 percent of Germans, 46 percent of the Irish, and 44 percent of Poles owned their own homes—figures that would have been virtually inconceivable in Europe at the time, particularly in Ireland and (what was once) Poland, whose residents were often virtual prisoners of foreign powers.

## The Power of Homeownership

With the erosion of the corporate social contract, in the twenty-first century the home became the last sacred economic asset in America. That changed with the housing bust. The price of maintaining this asset may have become too dear, as witnessed by the meltdown that began in 2006. By 2008, taxes and other homeownership expenses had risen to unaffordable levels for millions. Many developments had turned into spurbs, areas of ex-urban cul-de-sacs that couldn't be sustained by current economic and natural resources. Now more than four hundred suburbs in twenty-four states are economically distressed, showing poverty rates 50 percent or more above the national average.

Many economic drivers were in place to create an ideal environment for exuberant speculation and economic decay. The historical, spiritual, and cultural groundwork had been laid a long time ago. Now all that was needed was for the numbers to line up. Many thought they did, but that was part of the increasingly unaffordable myth of American homeownership in the twenty-first century.

# CHAPTER 3

# How Debt Addiction
# Fed a Housing Crisis

THE LEGACIES OF John Law and Thomas Jefferson and the sanctity of American homeownership merged sometime in late 2002. Robert Shiller, an economist at Yale Law School, saw the dangerous fusion coming and sounded the warning. While the media and Wall Street analysts were extolling the unlimited virtues of housing, mortgages, and homebuilding stocks, Shiller stood by his home-bubble prophecy, ignoring the increasing home-investment delirium. The boyish-looking professor, already an international celebrity in the late 1990s for his best-selling book *Irrational Exuberance,* applied the knowledge and experience gained from observing the stock bubble to the housing market.

There were potent signs that this mania would wreak vast economic damage. Shiller was among a small group of critics outside of Washington, Wall Street, and Main Street who warned of the bubble years before it burst. I endorsed Shiller's concerns in several columns I wrote for Bloomberg News, starting in 2003. As with his observations on the dot-com bubble, Shiller became the savant of the home market, although his prophecies were largely ignored by home buyers, the banking and real estate industry, speculators, and Wall Street. As an astute analyst of the economic dynamics of the bubble, Shiller was simultaneously tracking the mass psychology of the boom. In addition to having expertise on market movements, he is a leading international expert on behavioral finance, a discipline that melds psychology with economics, decision-making, and management philosophy.

Phrases such as "homes are the most solid investment" and "this time is different" echoed from coast to coast at the height of the surge in home prices. As in past manias, the conventional wisdom was not only the perception, it was also the *reality* because the economic mantra of the time was "buy more; prices are only going up." Such a widespread belief created a feedback loop, Shiller said. Buyers, bankers, and brokers saw the steady escalation in prices in the media and convinced themselves that home appreciation was inevitable and without limits. The idea that millions were also speculating during this craze rarely entered the public dialogue, and if it did, it was discounted as a minor driver of home prices since the rally was national in scope.

It was Shiller's ironic exposition of Alan Greenspan's phrase "irrational exuberance" to describe the dot-com stock bubble of the late 1990s that led him to look even more incisively at housing. It was as if home buyers had lost all sense of economic reality as they bid up prices between 2001 and 2005. Why did home prices suddenly shoot far beyond a historical average? Shiller's discovery that home prices from 1890 to 2004 had risen only *0.4 percent* after inflation had little impact on places like Las Vegas or south Florida, where the percent increases in housing prices skyrocketed double digits at the height of the boom. That meant that the appreciation seen in the hottest markets was a "black swan," an outlying anomaly that couldn't be sustained. Market economics always demands a painful reckoning; extremes will be evened out by time, come down to earth, and return to a long-term average. Like Icarus, prices that soared too close to the sun would indeed prove to have wax wings.

## Sloppy Economic Thinking

Although he says he's been "humbled as a forecaster," Shiller saw the hard fall of the bust coming, observing three years before the collapse the behavior that accompanied the bubble mentality. "It was sloppy economic thinking," he says of those who didn't realize they were participating in a mania. "It was the nature of a bubble that led people to believe that capitalism is triumphant. It was a gold rush."

Shiller says he sensed a mass behavioral shift around March 2000, when the '90s stock-market surge came to an end. Like the twenty-seven bubbles since the Dutch tulip mania in the early seventeenth century, Shiller says, the housing craze—an 86 percent increase in real prices between 1996 and the first quarter of 2006—showed classic signs. The cocktail party chatter about which was the best tech company to buy stopped in 2000. Nobody was talking about the best napkin-based business plan for an Internet start-up.

The *zeitgeist* moved on to the next best thing, which in turn spurred the greatest boom in housing on record. Shiller calls the shift in investment euphoria a "social epidemic, where certain public conceptions and ideas lead to emotional speculative interest in the markets and, therefore, to price increases; these, then, serve to reproduce those public conceptions and ideas in more people." The "meme," or idea virus, spread from Miami to San Diego: Homes became the financial panacea of the middle class.

Expectations for housing were further amplified by Alan Greenspan and the Federal Reserve Board. Greenspan ordered eleven Fed interest-rate cuts in 2001. The Fed's benchmark rate then stood at 1 percent in an effort to blunt the impact of a recession, the September 11 attacks, and the dot-com meltdown. The Fed, charged with regulating banking system liquidity and stimulating conditions for full employment, aggressively pumped cheap money into the mortgage market. Like Wall Street, home buyers loved and embraced the leverage game. In a market where 50 percent gains were realized within a few years, a buyer could purchase a $200,000 house with only 10 percent down (sometimes no down payment was required), and then sell it for $300,000.

Emboldened by these stratospheric returns, if you were savvy, you then invested in multiple properties. The lowest interest rates in a generation led to an explosion of adjustable-rate mortgage offerings, which were tied to short-term rates. When borrowers could get loans as low as 4 percent, they jumped at them en masse, not only buying first or move-up homes, but also second homes and investment properties that they could "flip" as the housing rally fed on itself and shrewd investors realized they could walk away with a double-digit percent of profit in a matter of months. This was the reasoning the Faieta family followed (see Chapter 1). It was perfectly rational since there was no reason to believe that anyone could lose money in buying American homes. No one had in recent memory. Since we are hard-wired to focus attention on results from the immediate past, there was a built-in mental bias convincing us of the truth of the assumption that "homes can't lose money." But, as is always the case, no investment is immune from the dictum "past performance does not guarantee future returns."

Local bankers and brokers saw few problems in granting loans to those who had little or no money down since they shifted the *risk* of owning the mortgages to an investment bank or government agency. The George Bailey approach seen in *It's a Wonderful Life* in which the local savings and loan financed neighborhoods—"your money's in Joe's home"—and kept the loans for thirty years went out the door in this new era of cheap money and securitization. In many areas, the increased supply of credit directly contributed to home-price appreciation. With cheap, accessible mortgage money—even to those who normally wouldn't have qualified for a loan—the opened floodgates of credit created buyers and inflated prices.

Mortgage brokers and bankers had little reason to worry about the oversight of local financing since they were loosely regulated and paid upon closing. They reaped billions based on volume, not borrower credit ratings. Once they sold a mortgage, they had no further obligation to ensure that the borrower could make the payments—especially if interest rates rose. Was credit becoming more democratic or was it a sucker's game where somebody would be left holding the bag when the market collapsed? Only a handful of observers such as Shiller suspected a con game was afoot.

## Wall Street's Bonanza

Each basket of mortgages reaped another fee for the investment bankers, who had no worries since the historical default rate on home mortgages had typically been well under 1 percent. But in keeping with the manic tenor of the times, Wall Street, too, got sloppy in its thinking about risk management. Many of the so-called "tranches" of debt *concentrated* some of the riskiest subprime and "Alt-A" mortgages into separate vehicles—although far too many bankers didn't seem to know it or acknowledge the dangers at the time. As Paul O'Neill, the outspoken former Treasury secretary, put it, "If you have ten bottles of water and one bottle has poison in it, and you don't know which one, you probably wouldn't drink out of any of the ten bottles." Wall Street not only drank the toxic debt in large quantities; by the end of 2008 it also would be forced to write down about $1 trillion (and counting) due to the bad paper.

From California pension funds to Norwegian municipal investment pools, the securitized debt from the housing bubble started strangling credit markets, from jumbo loans (mortgages for expensive homes) to student borrowing. Banks became ultraconservative in their lending, and even normally lax credit-card issuers started to get selective. The worldwide credit crunch was in full swing and would take years to unravel. Those who couldn't refinance during the meltdown when rates rose and standards tightened across the board hit a financial cul-de-sac and entered into a spiral of defaulted loan payments, foreclosures, and bankruptcies.

Chairman Greenspan repeatedly gave speeches in 2005 and 2006 as the growth expanded, insisting that there *couldn't* be a national real-estate bubble. Homes weren't like stocks, he countered numerous times. You couldn't buy and sell them in a day. They were largely illiquid. Transaction costs were high. There really wasn't a national real estate market. Greenspan's advice at the time: Get an adjustable-rate mortgage. *They* were a good deal.

## The Risk Shift: A Decayed Social Contract

Although Greenspan's legacy at the Fed underwent some unpleasant revision for his hand in the dot-com and housing bubbles, during his tenure he endorsed a long-term trend that encouraged the shifting of financial risk from one party to another.

Everyone in corporate America outside of the executive suite was feeling the pain. Hourly workers knew it most acutely. The middle class's economic footing was slipping in myriad ways, and cheap, dodgy mortgages seemed like a salve for many wounds. The social contract was in tatters as employers, over the past thirty years, shifted costs—and risks to their profitability—to employees. The decline of unionization and rise of the white-collar economy fueled the gradual risk shift.

For employers in the age of the 401(k), there was no need to set up and fund a large, expensive pension fund and guarantee retirement benefits when they could transfer most of the burden onto their employees through defined-contribution plans and save billions. Executives benefited most from this trend. Why would they pay for soup-to-nuts benefits packages when they could trim their bottom line, enhance their profit picture, and cash in their stock options at higher prices? Wall Street loved this idea and rewarded executives and stockholders handsomely for cutting benefits, future liabilities, and employees. The social contract was being rewritten by the managers of this new age. Freshly minted MBAs were retooling their spreadsheets to take corporate liabilities such as future retirement and health benefits off the balance sheet.

Jacob Hacker, a professor of political science at Yale, called the dissipation of the corporate social contract a "great risk shift" that created record levels of economic insecurity for middle-class Americans. Instead of being assured of upward mobility through income and benefit guarantees, Americans are exposed to even more market risks through their 401(k)s and adjustable mortgages as the economic seas are increasingly turbulent.

Plagued by ever-higher costs of living (particularly in energy and homeownership), "the incomes of middle-class families aren't much higher today than they were in the 1970s," Hacker stated. "Americans may be willing to turn a blind eye to growing [income] inequality, confident in the belief that their own standard of living is still rising. But economic insecurity strikes at the very heart of the American dream."

It was hardly a coincidence that the nadir of the housing crisis *and* the middle-class economic reversal occurred in 2007. The U.S. median family income slipped to $60,500 in that year. Only seven years before, families took home about $61,000, according to the U.S. Census Bureau. After the dot-com bust, they began to fall back. Americans largely knew they were receding economically and turned to their homes as fail-safe investment vehicles. They had few other choices.

## Can't Beat Inflation

Housing became a bulwark for individual investors because most financial assets were performing miserably in the first half-decade of the twenty-first century. From 2001 through 2005, large-company stocks returned a pathetic 0.54 percent. Even ultrasecure U.S. Treasury bills weren't worth bothering with, offering a 2.13 percent return adjusted for consumer inflation (at 2.49 percent for that period).

Most people were slaves to the relentless ogre of inflation: Housing costs, taxes, medical expenses, and college tuition were rising at double-digit rates in an era of single-digit salary raises. The cost of living for most folks was outpacing the government's official benchmark of the cost of living, the consumer price index (CPI). Wages were not keeping up with the bulk of it. Yet the CPI as a cost-of-living gauge was as useful as a wet finger in the air for precise wind direction. Since the U.S. Department of Labor doesn't even measure true homeownership costs—it tracks a rent-cost gauge—the consumer price index is vastly understated. Since the government uses the CPI to index Social Security cost-of-living increases, it has a vested interest in keeping it relatively low. So it's a convenient fabrication. The consumer price index is typically used as a benchmark for consumer inflation, though because of its horrendous understatement of the actual cost of living, it's not a reliable measure of what Americans are paying for big-ticket items.

Meanwhile, the so-called "ownership society" wasn't going so well for most folks. The promise of 401(k)-type defined-contribution plans providing adequate funds for retirement was fizzling. These vehicles for individual wealth were more likely to guarantee individual poverty as they replaced the employer-managed, forced savings defined-benefit plans that dominated the early years of the post-war boom. Employers provided little meaningful guidance on how to properly diversify with these plans or to absorb market shocks. Many of them were loaded with company stocks, another recipe for disaster in many cases. Almost none of them provided any form of guaranteed annuity. Middlemen and brokerage costs ate up returns in all but the largest programs. They were raw deals, although most Americans didn't have a clue as to how much these lame vehicles were costing them in terms of future retirement security. Congress dallied with various transparency measures to tell workers how much they were being gouged, although most were shot down by industry lobbies before they even got to floor votes.

In 1980, 92 percent of retirement contributions went into traditional defined-benefit plans, which peaked at more than 112,000 in 1985. Less than thirty thousand of these single-employer programs were still in effect by 2008. Most of those who are covered by them are with an old, mature company, in a union, or with a government agency. Unions represent about 12 percent of the American workforce, so the guaranteed, old-style pensions have been lost by most U.S. workers. Most employers won't offer them to new employees.

In the 401(k) world, neither a contribution nor a payment at retirement is guaranteed. Employers don't even have to offer the benefit. Employees are on their own to make their investment decisions, which for most people go the wrong way. Research by leading behavioral economists such as the University of Chicago's Richard Thaler shows that most employees make money-losing decisions in their 401(k)s: they either take too much risk or too little. Employers also do an inadequate job of educating their workers and pass along the costs of asset management, which eat into returns even further. As a result, the average per capita balance in a 401(k) for those retiring at sixty-five is about $30,000. The decaying social contract also offers less secure employer-provided health care. Many small companies don't even provide medical insurance, and four out of ten in the United States are small. More than 45 million Americans were uninsured in 2009; some 25 million were underinsured. And even workers at larger companies are facing an erosion of benefits. From 2001 through 2007, family health-care premiums rose 78 percent while wages increased only 19 percent and consumer inflation was up 17 percent. The average family pays about $12,000 a year for coverage, which wasn't the case a decade ago. As with retirement plans, employers have shifted cost increases onto their employees. Because wages aren't typically keeping up with benefit losses, families simply can't keep up.

The U.S. economy, though, was ever nimble and provided numerous ways of making up for the shrinking take-home pay and retirement kitties. It provided virtually unlimited credit during the housing boom years, some of it secured against the value of the home. By turning the domicile into a cash machine, Americans tapped into their home equity at rates never before seen. Unlike the generation that had lived through the Great Depression and relished the day when they could "burn their mortgage note," debt-encumbered baby boomers weren't seeing progressive rises in real income. Millions became addicted to this new-found source of money and concluded, "Why do I need a retirement fund; isn't that what my home equity is for?"

## Debt Addiction and the Tax Burden

The Fed's flood of cheap money during the housing boom fueled another mass economic malady: the "buffet effect." When any consumption item—whether it's food or money—is offered at one, low price, people tend to gorge on it. During the mortgage bonanza days, home buyers not only took out loans as if they were being given away, they took out second and third mortgages. They also tapped home equity by simply increasing the amount they were financing. Even down payments could be borrowed. By going deeper into debt, they felt as if they were "playing with the house's money," in Las Vegas patois. Homeowners were spending money that they thought was on the house; their loans were supposed to be covered by gains they bet would come in the future.

Homeowners were emulating their libertine Uncle Sam in their debt frenzy. The Bush administration and Congress were borrowing feverishly to finance income-tax cuts and the Iraq and Afghanistan wars. A national debt that was under $2 trillion in 1985 rose to more than $11 trillion in 2008. A budget *surplus* from the Clinton years evaporated. Much of the Treasury debt used to finance tax cuts and war materials was bought by the Chinese, who hold more than $1.6 trillion in U.S. debt securities. It hasn't been the greatest investment for them as the value of the dollar has sunk over the past five years, but it's bought them immeasurable good will.

The Fed was well aware of the debt excesses triggered by the bubble. Greenspan had documented the huge rise in home-equity debt during the bubble years. In a paper for the Fed cowritten with economist James Kennedy, he concluded, "Since the mid-1980s, mortgage debt has grown more rapidly than home values, resulting in a decline in housing wealth as a share of the value of homes." By 2008, Americans actually *owed* more on average than they owned in average home equity. While housing wealth had initially made Americans wealthier on paper, it also convinced them to save less and borrow more.

How could it be that homes were making people *poorer*? The answer was simple: Millions were going deeper and deeper into debt to finance their lifestyles and to keep up with bills. Not only did home equity provide a ready source of cash; for the bulk of Americans, it also was tax-free. If they withdrew funds from their 401(k), as millions did and are still doing as they exhaust their home equity, the money was subject to federal and state income tax plus a 10 percent penalty if taken out before age fifty-nine and a half. But home equity was sacrosanct in the tax code. You weren't subject to capital gains if your profit was under $500,000 (for married couples filing jointly) and it was from a principal residence that you lived in for two years prior to sale. Interest on home-equity loans was tax-exempt for the most part. And if you itemized on your tax return, mortgage interest and property taxes were deductible. Aided by the tax breaks, homeowners borrowed as much as they could.

So-called "equity taps" accounted for "four-fifths in the rise in home mortgage debt since 1990," according to the Greenspan report. How was this money being spent? In his typical tortured economic jargon, Greenspan cited "bridge financing for personal consumption expenditures." Translation: People were often buying boats, cars, and other items that would not increase the value of their homes. Ironically, while they were vacuuming about half a trillion dollars out of their homes annually from 1991 to 2005, the real U.S. savings rate turned negative.

Meanwhile, debt addiction spread to credit cards. "Plastic" debt has risen 31 percent since 2000, and tripled between 1989 and 2008. Those in the deepest credit-card trouble—some 20 percent of homeowners—paid off their unsecured plastic debt with equity from refinancing. They were paying off debt with more debt. Few in the outside world discouraged homeowners from their insatiable debt fix. Wall Street certainly made money from this addiction. The manufacturing, repackaging, and securitization of private debt reached epic levels as the twenty-first century dawned. Total credit-market debt topped $40 trillion in 2006, quadrupling from $10.5 trillion in 1987, which was the total for all private and public debt that year.

When they exceeded their limits on home-equity-related borrowing, highly leveraged homeowners loaded up on their credit cards: The average homeowner seeking foreclosure counseling in 2008 had about $17,000 in credit-card debt, up from $13,000 in 2006. The underlying driver of the constant demand needed to sustain the American economy is a debt bubble that threatens the global financial system. If it weren't for the fact that the United States is deeply indebted to Asia and Europe and their "dumping" of American debt securities would trigger the economic version of mutually assured destruction, the financial health of the last remaining superpower would be even more imperiled. The dark storm on the global economic horizon is that America's creditors are starting to move away from dollar-denominated debt into Euros and other currencies. That doesn't bode well for the debt-crazed U.S. economy.

It was not surprising that when the housing boom came along it provided another seemingly painless opportunity to borrow. With home prices rising, a consumer would need more money to buy a home anyway, and credit was available on easy terms. But the practice has only swelled homeowner debt burdens.

## Home Debt at Unsustainable Levels

During the 1990s, it took about 19 percent of monthly income to service the average conventional loan. By 2006, it took up to 37 percent of monthly pay. In coastal areas, homeowners were paying up to half of their income for a mortgage. What happened if homeowners got swamped by debt payments? If they couldn't afford the mortgage, they could sell the home and walk away. Or they could file for bankruptcy, which became tougher during the bust after a financial-industry-sponsored revision of the federal bankruptcy laws made it more difficult to discharge debts and start over.

At the height of the bubble, it was presumed a homeowner could even make a quick profit. So what if credit-card companies were hounding them? Credit-card debt is unsecured, meaning the companies couldn't take away a borrower's home if that person didn't pay. (The homeowner's credit record, however, was another matter; that would be wrecked.) And the home was where the cash was, so people availed themselves of the buffet.

The prospect that homeownership would forever free millions from the rental world went sour as *all* costs climbed during the boom years and into the collapse. "You have to cover home repair, heating and cooling, property taxes, and home owner's insurance—which rose 62 percent between 1995 and 2005—every month and every year, year in and year out," writes Nan Mooney in *(Not) Keeping Up with Our Parents: The Decline of the Professional Middle Class*. "Far from buying us freedom, the incessant costs related to ownership can leave us feeling under the financial gun for the rest of our home-owning lives."

Homeowners' financial obligations didn't end with their home-equity loans or mortgages. Gasoline prices, which soared above $4 a gallon in mid-2008, made it costlier to commute from the outlying areas that blossomed in the boom that were initially *more* affordable. It was costing more than $75 to fill up the SUV. The states with the greatest number of spurbs—California, Florida, Arizona, and Nevada—also had the highest rate of foreclosures. The coup de grace for millions during the housing bust was a quadruple whammy of higher adjustable rates, increased ownership costs, energy price increases, and higher property taxes.

## The Hidden-Cost Dragon: Property Taxes

The most overlooked truth of homeownership is that even if you manage to pay off a mortgage, you never really own your home free and clear. Property taxes come due every year. You don't have the option of avoiding them. Counties can slap liens on your home for unpaid taxes and can sell your property for the balance due.

The second most overlooked truth of homeownership is that even though you can chip away at the mortgage principal—provided you don't have an interest-only loan—if home values are rising, in most places, so does your property tax. There are, of course, exceptions such as California, where rates of assessed valuation are capped. In most other places, though, home assessments can rise infinitely. And it's an ownership expense that never goes away, often outpacing inflation and severely penalizing those on fixed incomes.

When home prices are rising, climbing property taxes almost always come with the territory (except in places where there is an extensive industrial and commercial tax base or an owner qualifies for a generous homestead exemption). After all, schools, fire and police departments, libraries, and forest preserves all have expenses that track inflation, too. If their property-tax revenue doesn't keep up with their budget increases, they have to tell taxpayers they are cutting back, which is never a politically popular option. Yet when property-tax hikes outpace salary raises, Americans fall behind in yet another way.

Even before the boom, the gap between rising property-tax bills and sagging incomes was hobbling middle-class homeowners, who likely borrowed more to meet their monthly bills. The difference in property-tax collections and incomes was stark during the bubble. In 2002 and 2003, property taxes rose by a factor of three relative to incomes, according to the Tax Foundation, a Washington-based taxpayers' group. Although the foundation's data extend only through 2004, real estate levies in most states continued to rise from 2005 through 2008, since taxes are based on a the average home values of previous years and assessed valuations are slow to be corrected by local assessors. The reason is that a sharp downward revaluation of properties would mean less income for local taxing bodies, which have fixed costs. While most states have limits on how much property taxes can rise during the good years, they are reluctant to lower taxes during a bust. That's why, despite the housing recession in 2008, state and local governments were still expected to collect a record $400 billion in property taxes, up from $326 billion in 2004, according to the U.S. Census Bureau.

Since assessed valuations were largely based on selling prices, those with the newest homes got hit the hardest if they bought during the boom and paid the highest prices. Meanwhile, it was unlikely that their incomes were keeping up with ever-increasing tax bills, particularly in spurbed areas in Arizona, California, Florida, and Nevada. All told, from 2000 to 2004, property-tax collections rose almost 30 percent while incomes grew only 16 percent. Most of the highest taxes were paid in the New York metropolitan area, with Westchester and Nassau Counties, New York, and northern New Jersey leading the pack, according to the Tax Foundation.

"Build it and they will come" was a costly proposition for most homeowners. In most states where there was a housing boom, property-tax demands increased simply because more infrastructure was needed to support the rising population. More fire stations, schools, libraries, and roads were built when the money was flowing during the boom years. Every taxing body adjusted their budgets upward based on the increasing revenue stream. But the lowering of property values, which began in 2007, didn't translate into lower property-tax bills since assessments can reflect an average of at least three years of past home values. The major pain for local and state governments will register soundly in 2009, when nearly every taxing body will either have to cut back on spending or raise taxes through their levies or referenda—if home values remain depressed.

During the bust, state capitols started to hear and act upon the despair of millions of homeowners aggrieved over property-tax bills. Indiana and Florida curbed tax bills. Idaho, South Carolina, and Texas employed tax "swaps" to replace property taxes to other levies. The Faieta family (see Chapter 1) felt the tax increases acutely, since they owned several properties in a declining market.

For the states, the bust meant more dire circumstances due to sharply diminished income, gambling, retail, and business tax revenues. At the end of 2008, nearly every large state was facing a budget deficit. California even appealed to the federal government—enmeshed in a financial industry bailout of its own—for aid. Home buyers who moved out to unestablished areas with new construction would face the worst local tax increases since these places had no solid tax base before the housing boom. In municipalities where price growth was most explosive, the declines in values and subsequent property-tax revenue during the bust were most pronounced. Prices in Los Angeles, Phoenix, and Miami doubled from 2002 to 2006, and then fell about one-third by the end of 2008. For those who stay in these areas, the eventual cutback in public spending may translate into a lower overall level of public services.

## Unlinking Property Taxes from Local Needs

Ralph Martire understands the relationship between property taxes and social progress better than most Americans do. A former corporate lawyer and executive director of the Chicago nonprofit research organization Center for Tax and Budget Accountability, Martire has led the charge for rethinking the way taxes are allocated. A municipality's tax base—the source of its tax revenue—needs to be diversified to be fair and to promote better distribution of revenue for education. Municipalities with substantial home values receive generous revenues for schools and other services. In poorer areas, the schools and other public services suffer.

"Money does matter," Martire says of the relationship between school quality and funding levels. "In Illinois, minority school districts start out with $1,154 less per child to spend on education than nonminority districts. That's the second-worst gap in the nation." Martire's reform plan in Illinois, which is echoing throughout the country, would garner taxes from a wider base, that is, from state income taxes, sin taxes (gambling, alcohol, cigarettes), and other fees. Local homeowners would then receive a break on their property-tax levies.

Neutralizing the expected dissent from above-average school districts, Martire's plan would not "Robin Hood" revenues by taking money away from the rich to give to the poor. The net result would be positive for homeowners. A lighter property-tax burden would raise property values without compromising school quality. The formerly underfunded districts would get more money. Since there's a strong relationship between educational attainment and future income, less-fortunate students would be able to obtain better jobs and boost their lifetime incomes.

Why does tax reform in the Land of Lincoln matter to the national housing market? Because property-tax realignment is not only necessary for making homeownership more affordable, it also fulfills a greater social need to provide more money for education everywhere. Better-educated Americans can become homeowners because they will earn more. But first state and local governments need to stem the rise in housing costs and begin to pay for growth through sources other than property taxes. The American dream of moving farther from a city to buy a bigger house and find better schools has become a costly proposition.

High-growth areas nearly always translate into higher property taxes. One study in Dane County, Wisconsin, where the tax burden is among the highest in the United States, showed that while the county's population grew 12 percent from 1990 to 1996, total property taxes soared 3.57 times faster than the population. Part of the reason is that developers rarely pay the long-term costs of building communities. Impact fees are often minimal.

Once subdivisions are built, builders are off the hook to fund schools, parks, roads, and other infrastructure. In fact, the disparity between what a single-family home costs taxpayers and what developers pay is huge. In Franklin, Wisconsin, just south of Milwaukee, each new home cost taxpayers more than $10,000 for schools and services in 1992 (it was considerably more by 2008). The developer's contribution: $813 per home. Impact fees vary from locale to locale, but they never cover the full cost of development.

Taxpayers feel the sting of property-tax increases even as home values recede. That's the bitterest aftertaste of the housing dilemma. It gets worse: As tax revenues plummet across the country, politicians from Florida to California are either cutting state budgets or asking for tax hikes.

Schools, which are the largest consumer of local tax dollars, went up like mushrooms during the boom. So it surprised no one that the total state and local tax burden hit a twenty-five-year high in 2007. *Growth was good.* That had been the mantra ever since Europeans set their lusty eyes on North America. Yet the myth spread by most policymakers that "growth pays for itself" was never true. Property owners almost always foot the bill for development through taxation. Homeowners usually get hit the hardest.

For most working families, one of the prime reasons to tolerate higher taxes is having more money for education. Paying a premium for a home translated into an above-average school system in most cases. Unfortunately, the burden of taxation and its inseparable link to school quality have pushed many families to the brink of economic ruin. Growth for them has come at a price. Two incomes were needed to pay the bills of that home in a prime neighborhood. Preschool children were dumped into daycare for ten hours at a stretch. Countless families who were one financial emergency away from ruin have already lost their dream homes in the bust. They mostly couldn't keep up with rising tax and homeownership bills.

Although state lawmakers will eventually gain more money from Obama's stimulus plan for big-ticket items like education and infrastructure, it won't change how homes are actually built or why they are *overbuilt*. Big new homes with large price tags will always be favored by local elected officials as long as home values and property taxes are directly linked to how much local schools and local government receive. They don't build McMansions in areas with impoverished school districts. Yet the demands of an energy-intensive global economy combined with a worldwide economic contraction and tightening of credit will make large homes in spurbs increasingly unaffordable.

The American dream home, which I explore in the next chapter, will have to be redesigned for this new reality.

# CHAPTER 4

# Cul-de-Sac Nation
## Symptoms of a Syndrome

ONE PERVASIVE PREMISE that circulated in the media during the housing bust was that homeowners brought on their collective misery *by themselves*. Wall Street wasn't to blame. The bankers and brokers were only providing a service that homeowners *wanted*. Then there was an accusatory tone that was directed toward home buyers. After all, many conservative pundits opined, "weren't people getting into more debt to buy McMansions? They weren't able to afford those places in the first place!" Some of this was true, although the real estate brokerage, building, mortgage, and investment-banking industries made billions on this premise.

In *House Lust,* author Daniel McGinn maintained that Americans got swept away by their obsession with new, shining palaces full of marble bathrooms and granite kitchen countertops. In detailing "real estate promiscuity," McGinn acknowledged that Americans relied on their homes as a retirement plan and got consumed by the bonfire of the vanities in using homes as status symbols. "We send signals by where we live—a piece of information that communicates socioeconomic rank as clearly as shoulder stripes denote status in the military. In America, homeownership has always been treated as a virtue."

Beyond the glamour of a big, castle-mimicking edifice, what price have Americans paid for the American dream? Several layers of crushing debt are the most obvious economic burdens. There's also the time spent away from child raising as both parents are needed to work to pay ever-higher tax, maintenance, and other bills. It can prove to be a disastrous economic family burden.

As Harvard researcher Elizabeth Warren and former McKinsey consultant Amelia Warren Tyagi discovered in their *The Two-Income Trap: Why Middle-Class Mothers and Fathers Are Going Broke,* "the average middle-class family can no longer afford to buy a home unless both parents work. . . . Even if they are able to trim around the edges, families are faced with a sobering truth: Every one of those expensive items we identified—mortgage, car payments, insurance, tuition—is a fixed cost. Families must pay them each and every month, through good and bad times, no matter what. Unlike clothing or food, there is no way to cut back from one month to the next."

Did Americans truly bring on economic calamity simply through wanting a better life and owning a home with more amenities? It's undeniable that new homes have gotten larger. From 1970 to 2005, the number of new homes with four bedrooms rose to almost four out of ten, reports the National Association of Home Builders, an industry trade association. More than 70 percent of home buyers wanted a garage and a large kitchen. And interior space increased to 2,400 square feet—a 62 percent jump. More space coupled with escalating land prices meant a higher median sticker price, around $225,000 (in 2007), and an average cost per square foot of $92 (nearly doubling from 1996 to 2008).

Growing incomes made much of this move-up mentality possible, and the ubiquitous availability of leverage financed it. Those who upgraded wanted to keep up with the Joneses. Keep in mind that the 1990s had been relatively prosperous for most Americans. Homeowners bought more house because they were confident their incomes would rise. The benefits of that rising tide ebbed more than a half-decade ago, and few saw the retrenchment coming. By 2008, nearly every commodity price had hit record highs due to supply problems, climate factors, and speculation. High energy prices affected everything from corn production to airline travel.

The great American home of the past is not tenable in a resource-challenged time. The size and resource consumption of the sacred castle has also hit a cul-de-sac.

## Energy Use and the Unsustainable Home

Rising energy prices will make large-lot suburban living that involves extensive vehicle travel economically unsustainable, a subject well covered in the work of James Howard Kunstler, the author of several books on suburban decline. The long-term view on energy availability, cost, and delivery is not bullish. Numerous energy analysts have reported that the world may have reached peak oil production, and it's clear that new reserves will scarcely meet the demand from the United States and developing nations such as China and India. Although energy prices abated in 2008 (oil prices slipped from $147 to below $40 a barrel) worldwide demand will far outstrip the supply if prerecession growth trends continue. Many analysts believe that world oil supplies will peak between 2010 and 2020. By 2030, demand may be as high as 120 million barrels. That means that a shortfall could cripple the global economy by 2015. That forecast is predicated on no significant new oil fields being found and no new economically feasible fuel alternatives coming along to replace oil.

Oil and fuel have not only gotten more expensive during normal times, they are becoming far less plentiful. Does that mean we'll start running cars on the abundant but environmentally catastrophic reserves of coal? If anything, Americans are moving in the opposite direction of an energy-stingy model. We will need even greater energy supplies to run the home of the future.

There's little for homeowners to be optimistic about on the energy front. Most people cringe at the prospect of $200-a-barrel oil, and its most obvious effects are felt at the gasoline pump, the airline ticket counter, or the bill for heating a home with oil. Soaring oil prices, though, are reflected in higher costs of food, all manufactured items, and transportation. These increases will change the American way of life as we know it. The "bigger is better, move farther out to buy a bigger home" ethos of the boom days is going to be the first victim of a new energy crunch.

Longer term, the energy-intensive lifestyle of big-house living has hit an economic cul-de-sac. Consider how much power it takes for the modern, infotainment-driven home. One or two color televisions have been replaced by several flat-panel, plasma, or LED screens. Radios and stereos have been displaced by multiple, networked computers with even more flat-panel monitors and a constant need for electricity (even when they're turned off). Add to that the plethora of other electronic devices, from video games to cell phones, and you have a home that devours exponentially more power than it would have twenty years ago. Plasma TVs alone consume up to four times more power than older, cathode-ray models.

## The Gluttonous Wired Home

According to energy expert Robert Bryce, "All of those new electronics have helped continue to drive electricity demand ever upward. In mid-2007, electricity demand was growing by 2.7 percent a year. If demand continues growing at that rate, electricity consumption in the United States will double in about twenty-six years."

All of those remotes and the appliances they control really add up. A handheld battery-operated device, multiplied by millions, may be part of a collective weapon of mass destruction. Power needed to run electronics must be created by plants that produce mammoth amounts of carbon dioxide, mercury, and smog-producing chemicals. We breathe that tainted air and water. Miners and mountains die while bringing the coal to the surface.

What the energy planners don't quite know is where all the new power for the growing electronic gadget mania will come from; the electrical grid capacity isn't sufficient and there is likely to be a gap of about 81,000 megawatts by 2015. That's an equivalent of the output of ninety-five nuclear reactors, Bryce estimates. The ever-greater reliance on Internet-based services does save on energy. People can shop, play games, download movies, and even do financial planning on the Web without getting into a car. But the Internet and computer-driven services also use an awful lot of power.

Computer servers consume about 1.2 percent of all U.S. power, or about as much as all the color TVs in the country. It's estimated that Internet colossus Google alone consumes as much power running its computer servers as eleven thousand homes. And with the incredible breakneck rise in the popularity of sites like Facebook, YouTube, MySpace, and countless others, Internet power needs will only continue to grow. Being connected 24/7 eats up a lot of juice, most of it flowing directly into our homes.

## An Outdated Grid

Normally, worrying about home and online power consumption is a wonkish concern best left to government and utility analysts. After all, what can an average homeowner do about expanding the power grid? The grid wouldn't be a problem if the energy supply was keeping up with demand. It isn't and will be a huge infrastructure barrier in the future for every homeowner, even with the Obama administration's planned upgrades.

The North American grid is antiquated and prone to blackouts, as witnessed by the massive August 14, 2003, shutdown that darkened cities from Detroit to New York. The system can't efficiently deliver power to where it's needed—most energy is lost in the transmission and generation process—and needs anywhere from $56 billion to $450 billion in new investment to make it "smart" enough to handle the growing needs of the information age. And that doesn't include the need for new power plants. One estimate indicates that eighty-three new plants are needed by 2020 to keep up with the demand; about 150 coal-burning plants are planned.

With global warming concerns, building new dirty coal-fired stations garners little support outside of the power industry, although it is the dominant technology in the world and in twenty-five states. The newly built plants will have extensive pollution controls, but they still produce copious amounts of carbon dioxide, which contributes mightily to climate change. The new generators may likely be subject to carbon taxes, making the power they generate even more expensive. Natural gas–fired plants are cleaner than coal—and methane is still relatively plentiful in North America—but they still produce carbon dioxide. Nuclear plants are much cleaner, but they cost more, generate nuclear waste that needs to be transported and stored in a secure location, and are still politically unpopular, although they're gaining more currency because they don't generate greenhouse gases.

The only conclusion that nearly every energy analyst can reach is that the cost of central station electricity is going up and the age of cheap power may be over. It climbed about 10 percent in 2006 alone during the height of the housing boom; that ascent was about three times the rate of inflation. A record number of homeowners applied for energy-bill assistance after the winter of 2007–2008. In a time of stagnant wage growth, energy inflation will make homeownership even more costly. The fuel used to create electricity costs more, resulting in power prices going up as much as 30 percent.

One other energy-related issue that is rarely discussed is that most power generation requires incredible amounts of water, another resource that is in dwindling supply.

## Water, Water Everywhere? Not Anymore

The Atlanta area defies geographical description. It starts out somewhere
at the base of the Appalachian range south of Chattanooga, Tennessee,
and wanders in all directions until you reach the piney woods of central
Georgia. When I drive through Atlanta on I-75, I am always struck by
the lushness of the metropolitan region of more than five counties. Yet
the appearance of the dense forests and generously landscaped subdivisions and office parks gives way to another reality that plagues far too
many American population centers: the consumption of unsustainable
amounts of water. As with power, the demand exceeds the supply.

I drove through Atlanta twice during my research tour in 2007, when
the capital of the South was still building in every direction. In-city
developments such as Atlantic Station, the site of an old steel mill, were
being reclaimed and thoughtfully restored as were other neighborhoods
within the city. Office parks built in clusters on the perimeters of the
highways that ring Atlanta were continuing to grow. Homes were being
built farther and farther out to ensure that there was a price point for
everyone's new castle. Not surprisingly, more than half a dozen Atlanta-
area counties appeared in the U.S. Census Bureau's list of fastest-growing
areas during the boom years.

The summer of 2007, however, saw a drought in Atlanta that would
highlight an Achilles heel in the growth prospects of any area that is
water challenged. Not only would homeowners, office buildings, and
commercial landlords be forced to conserve, they also would be limited
in the amount of additional electricity they could obtain. You can't have
conventional power without water. Electric utilities now consume about
20 percent of all water in the United States. Three times as much water
is required to generate power for the average home than is collectively
used for toilets, washing, and watering the lawn.

Growth depends directly on regional water supplies. Since it also
takes water to scrub pollutants from coal-fired generators, newer plants
are likely to consume up to 60 percent of nonfarm water. Water use in
power generation uses up to 480 gallons per person per day in states that
don't have hydroelectric dams or seawater-cooled plants. That's not a
problem if government can increase the supply of water. Unfortunately,
the amount of accessible fresh water is finite and being used up faster
than it can be replaced. Although water covers about 70 percent of the

planet's surface, less than 1 percent of it is available for human use. Of the surface water that's available, the lion's share is in the Great Lakes and is unavailable to coastal regions.

## Groundwater Gone

In far too many places, groundwater is fairly tapped out. The Atlanta area relies upon Lake Lanier as a reservoir, which was in danger of going dry in the summer of 2007. Without stringent and consistent conservation measures, the combination of a drought and excessive use can be catastrophic. At the height of the drought, newspapers published a list of the most egregious water consumers in the Atlanta area. In suburban Atlanta, some homeowners were consuming hundreds of thousands of gallons—a day. The state of Georgia started a legal dispute with the state of Tennessee over the location of state boundaries so that Atlanta could tap more water. Georgia, Florida, and Alabama have sued each other over the use of water from the Apalachicola River basin.

Upscale American suburban life is water intensive. Lawns, landscaping, swimming pools, and Jacuzzis can easily use thousands of gallons. Contrast that with the typical household average consumption of about four hundred gallons per day for ordinary activities. The bigger the house and lot and the more water-intensive amenities it has, the more water the owner uses. And it's not just homeowners who are water-intensive consumers. One of Atlanta's biggest employers and the largest beverage company in the world—the Coca-Cola Company—uses more than 283 billion liters of water every year. What will global warming mean for groundwater availability? Some areas will get more rainfall, ironically. But arid areas that have been subject to droughts may continue to have water shortages.

Although the drought brought worldwide media attention to Atlanta in 2007—when it seemed liked a rare, isolated event—water shortages have been a persistent problem in the area over the past century. It experienced droughts in 1903–05, 1930–35, 1938–44, 1950–57, 1980–82, 1985–89, according to the U.S. Geological Survey, which monitors water conditions throughout the country.

You don't have to go far from Atlanta to find water shortages. Coastal communities in rain-rich Florida are now forced to desalinate seawater to replace the fresh water from the once-abundant aquifer that's been pumped dry in many areas. The Southwest from Texas to southern California is perpetually threatened by drought.

Perennially parched southern California was fretting that the Sierra Mountain snowpack was 67 percent of normal in the spring of 2008. That translated into a water shortage for southern California, which pumps most of its water from the mountains in the north-central part of the state (and the strained Colorado River). New housing development hit a wall in 2008 as California builders started to lose their ability to win building permits because of a state law that required them to prove that they had access to twenty years' worth of water. It seemed to be more than a coincidence—perhaps a metaphor—that the communities hardest hit by foreclosures were in the hottest and driest parts of the state, from Riverside and San Bernardino counties in the south to San Joaquin in the north. This dilemma plagues the arid West every year in addition to increasingly frequent wildfires. Similarly afflicted communities in Las Vegas and Phoenix also face water shortages.

Many states suffer from water woes. The U.S. government's "drought monitor map" showed distressed water conditions throughout most of the West, including the mountain states; in the Southeast; and even in unexpected places like the Great Plains, the Mississippi River Valley, and parts of New England. The Colorado River basin has been experiencing a drought for *eight* years. All told, thirty-six states—more than half of the country—are expected to face water shortages by 2013, "even under nondrought conditions," according to the U.S. Environmental Protection Agency.

Of the 345 billion gallons used in America in a single day, agriculture consumes the largest share, followed by electric power generation and domestic use. Yet population growth inevitably means more homes needing more power and water (in addition to more food). In Florida alone, some 9.3 billion gallons a day will be needed in 2030. That's 30 percent more water than the state has access to today. "The U.S. is heading toward a water scarcity crisis," says Robert Glennon, the author of *Water Follies,* a classic examination of water shortages. "Our current water use practices are unsustainable, and environmental factors [global warming, droughts] threaten a water supply heavily burdened by increased demand."

Unless the climate unexpectedly and mysteriously shifts so that arid areas are watered and groundwater supplies replenished (it doesn't seem to be working out that way thus far), cities like Las Vegas, El Paso, Phoenix, and Albuquerque could run out of water. Even hydrologic heavens in the Midwest and New England will see problems if groundwater dries up. Conservation has never been more important. Las Vegas is paying homeowners $2 a square foot to pull up grass. Dozens of communities are building reclamation facilities to recycle wastewater.

Even more than energy, water may be the defining resource issue of the global economy in the twenty-first century. Some 2 billion people on the planet don't have access to fresh water, and some of the most pronounced problems are in places like China, where industrialization is consuming vast quantities that can't be replaced. The U.S. population alone is expected to grow by another 129 million people by 2050. Where will the water come from? Will it be available to fill McMansion swimming pools and water landscaping? Mother Nature isn't making any more bodies of fresh water, and it can't be mass produced like tract homes.

## Unpaid Infrastructure Bills

Keeping the lights on and the water flowing from the tap are related to more egregious problems in public financing and planning. Congress and state governments are simply not keeping up with infrastructure development, maintenance, and repair. The basic support systems of our everyday world are crumbling, and we're not spending enough money to fix them. Sadly, Congress placed a higher priority on giving tax breaks to the well-heeled during the Bush years than devoting dollars to water-treatment plants, pollution control, bridges, and the electrical grid.

The gap between what needs to be done and what Congress is spending is about $1.6 trillion over the next five years, according to the Urban Land Institute. That's a paltry 0.93 percent of the U.S. gross domestic product (as of 2007). Contrast that with India, which is spending 3.5 percent of its budget on infrastructure, or China, which is doling out 9 percent. Granted, these countries are largely undeveloped and growing faster than the United States. But policymakers' widespread neglect is creating a growing bill that can't be ignored in an age of increasing resource scarcity and higher energy prices. The Obama administration and Congress will address some of this funding gap, although it will take decades of spending to update the infrastructure from coast to coast.

Suburbs have soaked up more than their share of infrastructure dollars. How do most homeowners get to their ex-urban Valhallas? They drive, which means new highways, streetlights, curbs, gutters, and related improvements. Most of this work was federally financed with tax dollars and debt: Congress set aside about $300 billion for road construction in its last massive highway bill (only $45 billion of that total was earmarked for mass transit). When you move away from an urban center, you *expect* there to be adequate road access. Part of the affordability quotient is that state and federal governments largely subsidized the choice to drive to a place that was formerly a farm field or desert. In addition to writing off taxes, mortgage interest, and capital gains, suburban homeowners benefit from infrastructure financed by state, local, and federal taxes. Although the price of a home drops 1.5 percent to 6 percent for every mile you're willing to drive, eventually you *will* pay higher taxes on every level (including tolls and higher water and power fees). Again, growth never paid for itself and household income hasn't kept up with paying for it.

The housing boom added to state and municipalities' fiscal misery. To afford larger homes in decent school districts, home buyers were willing to extend their commute to outer suburbs bursting with new subdivisions. Their initial cost savings from buying a less-expensive home with more square footage and an outsized lot were obscured by the total costs in financing their dream locale.

A sewer line to a new "greenfield" development costs about $1 million a mile to build. For a low-density community of forty homes, it costs the municipality $25,000 per house. Let's say a builder built four hundred units instead of forty. Then the cost per home drops to $2,500. Of course, few new developments feature high density (and newer municipalities discourage them); they are dominated by single-family homes on large lots. Because towns have to build in new infrastructure to seed development, it's the costliest way of building. A New Mexico study found that a suburban home in a fringe area needed $22,000 in infrastructure improvements, compared to an in-city home cost of $1,000 per unit.

Usually there's no public transportation infrastructure where a homeowner builds a dream house. That's the case in most suburbs, where the auto rules. The suburbanite pays an average of $8,000 a year to own and maintain a car in after-tax dollars. There's no tax break unless the vehicle is used for business. There are no write-offs for commuting costs, period.

Need two or three cars? Double or triple that amount. Have a long commute? You'll pay more in fuel, insurance, and tolls. Transportation soaks up one-fifth of the family budget in most American households, an amount second only to housing costs. When the price of gasoline rises, that portion increases. Although Americans were patronizing public transportation in record numbers in 2008, that choice triggered another fiscal question: Where will the money come from to fix, maintain, and expand the mass transit infrastructure? From riders and taxpayers, of course (Obama's stimulus plan will help somewhat).

How far behind is America on its infrastructure bills? According to the American Society of Civil Engineers, which did a report card early in 2009, here's how it breaks down:

➤ Drinking water and wastewater treatment is underfunded by $400 billion (over the next twenty years). Taxpayers will need to pay higher water rates to fund these improvements.
➤ Poor road conditions cost Americans $67 billion a year in repairs. More growth means more roads, more repairs, and more traffic.
➤ Bridges are in dire need of repair. Nearly one-third are structurally deficient, and it will cost $17 billion a year over twenty years to fix them all. This item is nonnegotiable and has been put off too long.
➤ Although power demand has increased, maintenance funding has decreased 1 percent annually since 1992 and may need as much as $1.5 trillion by 2030. "The existing transmission system was not designed to meet present demand, which could result in increased electricity costs and greater risk of blackouts."

## Getting Off the Road

Because most of the new development over the past half-decade—the peak of the housing boom—was so vehicle dependent, it introduced a bevy of additional expenses and loss of productivity and time. From 1977 to 2001, the number of miles driven by Americans rose 151 percent. That's four times greater than the population growth, according to the *Wall Street Journal*. Not only are commutes longer—remember Americans moved farther away to be able to afford that *better* home—driving time may grow by an additional 50 percent between 2005 and 2030.

The estimated tab for all of this time sucked down a black hole is an estimated $78 billion annually. That's time lost sitting in traffic. It's nice to have an iPod and be able to call anyone on your cell phone (some even watch DVDs), but it's certainly not quality time spent at home or productive time in an office. You can't hug your kids, coach their soccer games, or check your mother's pantry while languishing in traffic. Long commutes are definitely not family friendly. They will either get shorter or force more people to take public transportation as energy prices climb and remain high. That is, if state and federal governments even make a long-term commitment to expanding public transit options when energy prices dip.

An equally troubling question concerns our health: What is all of this driving back and forth doing to our bodies and well-being? The cul-de-sac life is hardly an advertisement for a healthy suburban lifestyle, although the American dream peddlers sold that house in the country on the myth that it's a *healthier* place to live. The pursuit of happiness isn't all it's cracked up to be when you have a killer commute.

# CHAPTER 5

# The Spurbing of National Health

As NEARLY EVERY metropolis expanded, Americans regarded ex-urban living as a route to a healthier lifestyle. For centuries, the gentry have been able to escape the compacted, often-pestilent cities to their country retreats in attempts to avoid plague, cholera, typhus, and tuberculosis. The air and water were cleaner in their pastoral retreats. The food was fresher. The open vistas were believed to provide a spiritual, mental, and physical renewal not available in the sooty, manure-clogged streets of the nineteenth century. That was how some of the original planned suburbs such as Riverside, Illinois, and Radburn, New Jersey, evolved. Cities then were an unmitigated menace to public health.

Until 1900, for example, Chicago's drinking water supply, drawn from Lake Michigan, was tainted with slaughterhouse offal; epidemics were rampant. Even though the lake was the largest source of fresh water within the country, the fetid Chicago River flowed into it, carrying the city's effluence (city engineers cleverly reversed the flow of the river, sending sewage down the Mississippi River basin). Many other cities simply had wells that were absorbing waste from open sewers. Coastal cities dumped their sewage into the ocean. Outside of cities, you could tap water from a (usually) unpolluted groundwater well or other body of water. The prospect of suburban living not only echoed Jefferson's pursuit of happiness and Locke's desire for property protection, it also often ensured a longer lifespan.

The suburban growth era has reversed myriad advances in health care and longevity. Because we need to drive more to reach our destinations—whether it's work, shopping, or recreation—collectively we're adding to the overall pollutant load in the air and water. The transportation sector is responsible for more than half of all air pollution and it's getting worse. America and most urbanized countries have hit the same public health cul-de-sac: How do you reduce pollution if traffic keeps increasing because people live ever farther away from cities to be able to afford homes?

When the Clean Air Act of 1970 was passed, it was a landmark law that established air-quality standards for cities. Although air quality has improved somewhat, vehicular traffic continues to set records and urban air is getting worse again. When the law was updated in 1990, only fourteen cities out of 207 examined showed a reduction in smog, the noxious haze that is created by sunlight and a mixture of pollutants. More than 170 areas have experienced *no* significant reduction in pollution while twenty-five got worse. The most sprawling areas have unsafe air, according to the EPA's standards. They include Atlanta, Gary-Chicago-Milwaukee, Dallas–Fort Worth, Houston, Los Angeles, New York–New Jersey, Phoenix, San Diego, San Francisco, and Washington, DC. All told, some 159 million Americans live in bad-air metropolises.

The worsening air quality may partially account for the deadly rise in cases of asthma, the fastest-growing chronic disease. Minority children in the city are hurt the most, and the rate of increase has doubled over the past twenty years for children under four years. Smog and other pollutants act as an irritant to lungs, causing shortness of breath, wheezing, coughing, and in some causes death when the bronchial tubes constrict. The rate of death from asthma attacks—about fourteen daily—is three times greater than it was twenty years ago. It's now rare for anyone not to know someone suffering from asthma. I know several family members and neighbors who are afflicted.

While some asthma can be traced to indoor air pollutants and biological factors such as mold and pet allergens (researchers aren't sure how much), there's little debate that outdoor air is worst around highways. And this filthy air drifts into schools, playgrounds, public spaces, and even our homes. Long-term exposure also contributes to higher incidence of emphysema, pneumonia, heart disease, and other chronic respiratory conditions. One-half of all cancers that are caused by outdoor air toxins are released by vehicles, which expel some 3 billion pounds of carcinogenic chemicals per year.

We know that the air we breathe on the road is filthy. All you have to do is follow a truck belching diesel exhaust or a clunker that appears to be burning coal. Smog is visible in the distorted sunsets of every urban area. Yet we endure it, running the risk of contracting one or more dreadful diseases. In far too many areas, we drive because it's the only way to get somewhere. Urban planners, developers, and politicians gave us no choice. The American dream is not only costing us more money; it's costing us our health. Getting behind the wheel always had the potential of being hazardous to our health and well-being. It's clearly not getting any better.

## Driving Ourselves Sick

In the mature cities of the East and Midwest, it was (and still is in many cases) easy to get around. Workers lived close to a trolley, subway, bus, or commuter rail line. They didn't need to worry about traffic, parking, or the travails of getting behind accidents or being delayed by bad weather. Most city neighborhoods had their own unique shopping districts, libraries, schools, and often factories within walking distance. Thousands of people lived in a square block and kept these services alive through consistent demand. Yet when jobs left cities, neighborhoods started to decay and middle-class residents left for the suburbs in droves. They traded subway tokens for car keys. Where many families had been able to comfortably survive with one car (or none), they now needed two. Their places of employment moved out as well in many places. Those who couldn't afford to live near the verdant suburban office parks stayed in or near the city.

In the spurb era, virtually every new destination required a car; there was no public transportation created to serve the outer-ring suburbs that nearly escaped the orbit of the big city. In the great migration of jobs from blue-collar inner cities to white-collar suburbia, core cities became big losers of human capital. Everywhere outside of central cities involved a drive and a mammoth parking lot. Malls replaced neighborhood and downtown shopping districts. Downtown multistory department stores, open-air shopping centers, and local merchants in old town centers mostly faded away (more on this in Chapters 8 and 9).

It may well be true that we shop until we drop. The combined effects of driving to shop, work, eat, and recreate have taken their toll on our health, time, well-being, and family life. The average American driver spends 443 hours per year behind the wheel. That's the equivalent of fifty-five eight-hour days. A decade ago, when I was doing an "extreme" commute that often took me two hours one way in bad weather, I logged some fifteen thousand miles a year in my car. It was a lonely journey that hurt my marriage.

Between 1980 and 1997, the number of miles driven rose almost 70 percent. Where were we going? Mostly to work and back as we moved farther out from the city and from established modes of public transportation. In 2008, commutes averaged more than forty-five minutes for one out of every six Americans. What used to be a quick jaunt to the train station or the next community over became travel between counties, as it is in Atlanta, Chicago, Dallas, New York, Los Angeles, St. Louis, San Diego, and San Francisco. The number of extreme commuters—those traveling more than ninety minutes each way—described more than 3.5 million motorists, which was double the number in 1990 stuck in a car for that length of time.

It's not unusual for car commutes to be virtually the *only* way out-of-town homeowners can get to their jobs. Ringed by an interstate perimeter, Atlanta is defined by its highways, where some 94 percent of residents commute by car. The Athens of the South isn't all that unusual, though. From 1960 to 1990, the percentage of commuters with jobs outside their counties rose by 200 percent.

A long-term trend in employment has shifted jobs to suburban areas where land is cheaper. Manufacturing areas that were typically within five miles of an urban core are now farther out—and in far too many cases out of the country. Older industrial districts needed to be near rail lines, city infrastructure, and public transportation. New white-collar office parks needed only highway exits and infrastructure, both of which were often provided by generous federal, state, and local subsidies. As noted in Chapter 3, the lion's share of the federal transportation budget went to laying more asphalt, not public transportation, so Washington consistently subsidized the proliferation of highway madness and unhealthy environments.

Despite access to the Internet, phones, iPods, and other electronic media, people spend more time in a car, which means they spend less time doing other things, such as exercising and walking. The car-bound person may be prone to higher rates of chronic disease as a result. Even if weary commuters were able to get outside when they got home to walk around, where could they go? They can't walk to do errands from most subdivisions without having to ford a busy highway. It's just plain dangerous. American pedestrians and cyclists are up to six times more likely to die than their Dutch or German counterparts, who have more areas designated for walking or for bike lanes.

## Obesity Linked to Driving

The bulging of American waistlines paralleled the expansion of suburbia. One study found a direct relationship between body mass index (the amount of fat on your frame) and a measure of sprawl. Higher body mass and obesity correlated highly with areas where you mostly had to drive everywhere. Suburban car commuters also tend to stay in more, watch TV, and become more sedentary. The Centers for Disease Control and Prevention estimates that 200,000 premature deaths may be linked annually to the inactivity that is part of a car-dependent lifestyle.

When there's a fatal train or plane crash, which is extremely rare in the United States, it gets worldwide media attention. Yet the vastly more dangerous form of transportation is driving. More than forty thousand Americans are killed every year in vehicle accidents, or one every eleven minutes. Notable safety gains have been made over the years from the smallest subcompact to the largest semi-tractor-trailer (thank you Ralph Nader), but the advanced vehicle protection systems often give drivers a false sense of security—so they drive even more. Between 1982 and 2007, although the U.S. population grew 20 percent, vehicle miles driven climbed more than 236 percent. And the $200 million the government spends each day to add and repair roads only resulted in more traffic. Build it and they will come. Most roads are free; well, at least they don't charge tolls. You've already paid for them through your income and gasoline taxes and through profligate congressional and local borrowing. And homeowners continue to pay with their health, well-being, and lost time.

It can be argued that all of the money spent on roads makes our collective lives worse. Although road capacity was increased the most in the 1990s, time spent in traffic rose 70 percent. That time is spent in health-damaging inactivity and breathing poisons from vehicle exhaust (unless you choose to breathe stale recirculated air on your commutes).

Lung-related diseases from overcommuting may cause an estimated one hundred and twenty thousand unnecessary deaths. Particulate matter from exhaust is believed to kill sixty-four thousand people every year. There are countless other nasty effects on our cardiovascular, muscular-skeletal (back problems, anyone?), and mental health, but I think I've made my point.

Car commutes are killing people, but most ignore the risks so that they can have that castle in the country. The millions who overleveraged to get their piece of sod may be wondering if they're wasting their lives on the road. I know I asked myself that question when I was in the middle of it. It was a purgatory that I eventually escaped.

## Changing Direction

Can homeowners discover the road to physical, financial, and spiritual health? Many who've studied the issues have high hopes that by reinventing homes and communities we can turn the corner and make housing more affordable in the process.

Several allied movements in "sensible" or "smart" growth are taking a comprehensive planning approach to building (see Chapters 9 and 10). With these pioneering urban planners, architects, and developers, the cul-de-sac subdivision is a thing of the past. An offshoot of these movements is New Urbanism, a coalition that is refashioning every new project to promote walkability, reduce vehicle traffic, and increase building density (more on this cadre in Chapter 10).

An increase in density—that is, the number of housing units per acre—has a tendency to reduce traffic and pollution. The benefits are tangible. Doubling density in San Francisco, Chicago, and Los Angeles resulted in lower overall vehicle traffic, one of the benchmarks for successful New Urbanism. It was healthier, too. Emission of the three major pollutants associated with vehicle exhaust also dropped in more-dense areas. The matrix of solutions in many cases was simple: Put shops and homes closer together. Build narrower streets. Locate close to stops for public transportation.

Get people walking more and out of their cars, vans, and SUVs. It's a deceptively simple and elegant theme but so hard to implement in the spurbs. Still, consider some of the enormous estimated benefits: If Americans spent thirty minutes a day walking or biking to their destination, they could shed 3 billion pounds of flab. Have we gotten to the point where far too many of us die in auto accidents or from heart and lung disease or diabetes simply because we wanted that chateau in strip-mall land? Our lives won't be measured out in coffee spoons; they will be measured out in vehicle miles.

No matter how you examine it, the spurbing of America is unsustainable. The health problems that result from driving—and the pursuit of the American dream at any price—is shortening our lives. The insightful and feisty French philosopher Bernard-Henri Lévy calls our car-centric lifestyle a "social obesity." Traveling the country much the way his countryman Alexis de Tocqueville did in the 1830s and writing about it in the book *American Vertigo,* one of France's most incisive minds finds an "obesity of enterprises subject to the law of forced growth." Although I don't agree with all of Lévy's observations on American life, here's one that rang true:

> The bigger it is, the better it is, says America today. Large is beautiful, it repeats over and over in a kind of hysterical reversal of the 1960s slogan. A global total obesity that spares no realm of life, public or private. An entire society, that, from the top down, from one end to the other, seems prey to this obscure derangement that slowly causes an organism to swell, overflow, explode.

Is the overpowering lust for homeownership blinding Americans to becoming better world environmental citizens and improving our health? The most profound changes we can make will have to start with individual homes.

# PART 2

# Reinventing Home and Community

# CHAPTER 6

# Toward Sustainable Dreams

VICTOR ZADEREJ BOOTS UP his laptop to show me his spreadsheets as I nosh on a seafood taco in one of the countless theme chain eateries in Schaumburg, Illinois. He wants to reinvent the American home and has done the math to show me how much it will cost and the length of the payback time for the improvements he's engineered. As an engineer, he wants everything from the shell of a house to its heating and cooling systems to be redesigned for a world in which expensive crude oil (the oil futures price had soared beyond $137 a barrel by the second quarter 2008), global warming, and dwindling resources are facts of life. A retreat in oil prices triggered by a worldwide recession won't change the fact that growing populations will continue to place unsustainable demands on energy availability.

Zaderej first got the bug for home energy systems while studying at MIT in the late 1970s; it was the end of the turbulent decade of the Watergate crisis, oil price shocks, and lines at gasoline stations. Inflation was rampant, the stock market was dismal, and President Jimmy Carter had taken to wearing sweaters as a gesture to implore Americans to turn down their thermostats. He even installed electricity-producing solar panels on the White House to produce power (removing the panels was one of Ronald Reagan's first acts of office). An emerging Edison, with tousled hair and a penchant for calculating rates of return, Zaderej may have more of an impact on making the American dream home sustainable than a hotel ballroom full of architects, bankers, brokers, economists, and politicians.

Our meeting takes place in Schaumburg, a classic, energy-intensive spurb, formerly a farming community that morphed into mindless miles of shopping malls, parking lots, and highways. The vast majority of people access Schaumburg only by car. As an "edge city" of seventy-five thousand about twenty-two miles from Chicago, it lacks good mass transportation, and any noticeable charm. What it has is plenty of retail and office space and several exits on two different expressways that intersect near its shopping core. The lumbering cell-phone giant Motorola has its world headquarters here. Its parking lots would consume most American town centers. Yet it's representative of the places where more than half of Americans live and work and may be the most unsustainable kind of location economically when energy prices rise.

When Zaderej was in college, energy efficiency became a national obsession, spurred by the Arab oil embargo and subsequent oil- and gas-supply shortages. Americans were not used to waiting in long lines for gas. The world was actually awash with oil, and big consumers like China and India hadn't quite entered the picture as major players. One course, which captured Zaderej's attention at the time, prompted him to ask a basic question: What is the cost of conserving a barrel of oil for use in heating a home versus buying a $30 barrel of oil (remember this was during the disco era) to heat that same home? "What we found is that for $1.50 in 1980 dollars, you could save/buy a barrel of oil. The light bulb that went on in my head was, why would anyone ever spend any money on solar photovoltaics (solar panels that produce electricity), wind, etc., before they did everything possible to reduce the demand for energy in a home by proper design, that is, the best windows, heating system, and as much insulation as possible?"

It's been nearly thirty years since Zaderej asked that question. In the interim, he's had a thriving career making robots and circuit interconnects, and designing cell-phone antennae. He holds about thirty patents and has trademarked the term "attainable sustainable homes," which is the theme of his research and development model. As global warming concerns press creative thinkers to search for more ways to reduce carbon dioxide emissions, it's inescapable that much of that focus must be on buildings, which produce 30 to 40 percent of worldwide carbon dioxide emissions. American homes are notorious energy wasters, mostly because they are designed badly, use profligate resources, and have gotten larger. Their carbon footprints are elephantine, which is something Zaderej knows he can change with relatively simple technology.

## Scrapping Traditional Homebuilding

Zaderej is a true radical. He not only wants to do away with traditional stick building—walls of his homes would be made of prefabricated structural insulated panels (SIPs)—he sees houses of the future ranging from 1,000 to 2,500 square feet. It's a fairly anti-American notion that smaller is better, but he knows the math is pretty compelling because he can reduce the home's initial and ongoing price tag that way. One home he is working on will cost an estimated $110 to $120 per square foot. That's not bargain basement, but it's quite a deal considering the lifetime energy savings the home will generate.

Excessive energy use is one of many factors that have pushed the total cost of homeownership beyond the breaking point of untold numbers of American households. Every utility bill item has risen in the past five years, with few signs of abating. Electricity and water are in increasingly short supply as demand continues to rise. One of the rarely discussed demons of homeownership is how much utility bills have contributed to the unaffordability of American homes.

Fueling the cul-de-sac syndrome is the simple reality that the larger (and older) the home, the higher the energy bills. Homes heated by oil or propane get hit the hardest. As a fixed cost, utility bills are unavoidable. Something dramatic needs to happen if homeownership is to survive in a high-cost, energy-intensive time. We've already seen a preview of what happens when energy prices soar. As Bloomberg News headlined in mid-2008, "Wealth Evaporates as Gas Prices Clobber McMansions." The piece profiled a man living in West Virginia, who was commuting by car 120 miles round trip to his job in Washington, DC. Home prices in his neighborhood were dropping because of high gas prices. His four-bedroom home that listed for $360,000 in 2003 was now selling for $239,000. With global demand chasing after every new drop of oil, every gallon of fresh water, and every electron, it's unlikely that this malady will be cured soon.

## Energy Savings with Passive Houses

Inspired by the European "Passivhaus" concept, which originated as a way to cut home-energy costs, Zaderej did more than study how to reduce household energy consumption. He built a home from scratch in Oregon, Illinois, using passive-heating principles to see if it could be done—improving many details along the way and applying for patents for some of his ideas. This wasn't your typical dream house loaded with glitzy appliances, bathrooms the size of hotel lobbies, or air-conditioning units the size of jet engines.

Passivhaus dwellings use 80 percent less energy to heat and cool than conventional homes of the same size. More than six thousand of them have been built across Europe, but only a handful can be found in North America. The technical goal is stunningly simple: *Use one watt of electricity per every square foot of living space.* Most of the heat "collected" in these houses comes from the sun or the earth, which stays around fifty degrees when you go down about fifteen feet. Zaderej's version of the

Victor Zaderej's Pura Vida solar home
*Credit:* Victor Zaderej

Passivhaus, named "Pura Vida" (pure, or real, life—the motto of Costa Rica), uses less energy than conventional homes while supplying filtered fresh air and even temperatures throughout the house.

In practice, Zaderej needed the house to be an efficient solar collector able to distribute and store that heat. The earth's natural temperature provides geothermal air conditioning and some heat as well. Zaderej's 4,500-square-foot Pura Vida home employs natural thermal resources in an unassuming way. A slightly modified metal roof over the garage collects heat and channels it into a masonry wall in the office space above the garage. The heat can be pumped throughout the house. South-facing windows under eaves are designed to let heat in during the winter months that radiates into the floor and then warms the rest of the home. Supplemental heat is provided by a water heater and high-velocity ducts. Extensive insulation below the slab (eight inches of foam) and around the foundation prevent the winter's cold from entering the house.

What's remarkable about the home isn't the design: It looks like an unassuming house built into a hill with lots of south-facing windows. It's the *efficiency*. Zaderej employs a heating system that puts out a paltry 15,000 BTUs (British thermal units). About ten times that much is usually used in a conventional home of that size. His heating cost was $350 during the cold Midwestern winter of 2007–2008, which ran from November until May. Heating a similar nonpassive home could have cost more than five times that amount.

For a modest construction cost premium of 9 to 12 percent (or less if the homes are mass produced), all of Zaderej's building enhancements pay for themselves over time in energy savings. He likens the payback to that of a Toyota Prius, the high-mileage hybrid car that gets up to fifty miles per gallon on the highway with a combination of gasoline engine, electric motor, and batteries. None of his calculations figures on a quick return on investment. This is not a home for speculators. He expects to break even on his energy improvements over ten years and has figured that his energy savings will pay for the building cost three times over a century. "The Prius costs about 10 percent more to buy," he notes. "My house is like a battery system. It uses thermal mass as its heat storage. Architects don't know how to do this. They concentrate on the exterior look and not on whole house design. Energy costs are growing faster than inflation. Anybody would be able to afford this."

## Green Building for Healthier Homes

Deep in the heart of Ronald Reagan country, his home state of Illinois, I'm exploring why the housing boom created an environmental morass that deteriorates by the day. I'm back in Oregon, Illinois, touring the home of Kent and Kathy Lawrence, the couple who first insisted that I see Victor Zaderej's house, just a few miles northeast of where Reagan grew up. Zaderej first encountered the Lawrences when he and a friend (who looks strikingly like Microsoft founder Bill Gates) stopped to admire the Lawrences' windmill, which is at the entrance to their property. "Kathy happened upon them, saw 'Bill Gates' and a Toyota Prius with its MIT sticker and figured they were pretty harmless," Zaderej's wife Polly recalled. "So she stopped to talk and graciously invited them into her home."

The Lawrences' concern in building a home wasn't exclusively dominated by energy issues, although their home is energy efficient and has solar panels and a windmill. Indeed, their house is far from the hippie domes of the 1970s; it's an elegant, private house that harmonizes with the ancient oaks and undulating landscape of the Kickapoo Mud Creek Nature Conservancy. The healthfulness of the home and its surroundings fit in with their living philosophy, which they offer as a model for future homebuilders. With Zaderej, they are designing and building a separate green structure that will serve as an educational facility.

Like Zaderej's home, the Lawrences' home is not open to the public, although they frequently show it to interested parties who want to know about green homebuilding. Their meticulous attention to detail is evident in every material chosen and in their attempts to create a healthy indoor environment that uses resources moderately.

Kent, a Chicago lawyer who lives with Kathy in the city during most weeks, has airborne allergies that require that their homes have extensive filtration devices. The chemicals that the Lawrences sought to avoid are embedded within materials commonly used in several building products. Formaldehyde, for example, is a poison found in adhesives and bonding agents for carpets, particleboard, and plywood.

## Addressing Indoor Air Pollution

Most Americans have good reason to be concerned about indoor air pollutants, particularly in newer homes. Poor interior air quality, according to research by the American Lung Association, "can cause or contribute to the development of chronic respiratory diseases such as asthma and hypersensitivity pneumonitis. In addition, it can cause headaches, dry eyes, nasal congestion, nausea, and fatigue."

Although no one knows the extent of indoor air pollution, 90 percent of our time is spent indoors with about 65 percent of it at home. U.S. Environmental Protection Agency studies have found that interior pollutant levels can be two to five times higher than they are outdoors. Chemical concentrations can certainly be much higher than that when most paints, stains, varnishes, and cleaning products are being used.

Children are the most vulnerable to these poisons: They breathe in 50 percent more air per body weight than adults. Noxious indoor substances may trigger asthma, a disease that afflicts more people every year: 4.2 million children and about 8 million adults in 2008. Controlling exposure to indoor allergens and tobacco smoke could prevent 65 percent of these cases. Although lumped in with "sick" commercial and office buildings, ailments related to indoor pollutants are estimated to cost $58 billion annually in medical payments and lost productivity. Most newer homes emit potentially dangerous chemicals constantly, from seemingly benign surfaces such as carpets, walls, and ceilings.

To cut down on indoor chemicals, the Lawrences finished the interior of their Oregon home with low-VOC (volatile organic compound) coatings that are water based. The health of the land was also paramount to the Lawrences. They wanted something "that reflected our vision of a home surrounded by nature, one that would blend with nature and would minimally impact its surroundings." So when they built their modest country home, a resource ethic informed the design of the house. They built in a nature conservancy.

The Lawrences believe that their home, located about a hundred miles west of Chicago, doesn't unduly disturb the gentle sloping hills, tiny creek, and prairie. It's unassuming, without flat-panel screens in every room, high ceilings, or grand stairways. An intimate outdoor patio holds a wood-burning fireplace. A narrow deck along the back of the house looks out on the conservancy. At the entrance to the property, there's no gate or security checkpoint. You know you've arrived when you see the windmill.

## Custom Green

The Lawrences' choices echo a powerful trend in custom building, where green features are designed to create a healthier exterior *and* indoor environment. They insisted on recycled newspaper and cardboard insulation and on components that made the home stingy on energy use.

Although there's no exact tally of how many homes are being built employing healthy construction principles, green homebuilding surged more than 50 percent between 2004 and 2006, according to the National Association of Home Builders, a trade organization in Washington. Environmental construction may represent the only consistent pocket of growth in a market wracked by a housing downturn, foreclosures, and a credit crunch.

Green building not only represents a viable option for mainstream builders, it also could buoy an industry anchored by conventional cul-de-sac development, because this kind of building adds measurable value to the home and reduces ownership costs over time. Green homebuilding was a $2 billion industry in 2007 and is forecast to grow tenfold by 2010, according to McGraw-Hill Construction. Prompted by a combination of eco-chic and health and energy concerns, homeowners are also searching for durability. Green homes are typically better built than production homes because they use better materials and insulation. Houses that feature better protection against the elements last longer, are less vulnerable to rot and insect damage, and often require less maintenance.

Catering mostly to those who have a hefty budget, custom green homebuilders employ materials such as bamboo flooring and certified wood products grown in a sustainable manner. The list of green features is endless. You can order recycled glass tiles for kitchen and bathrooms. A pollution-free geothermal heating and cooling system can use buried tubes and a heat pump to use the earth's natural thermal mass. You can even recycle rainwater through storm-water retention systems for irrigation and build a driveway that rain can permeate. The sky's the limit— only your pocketbook limits your possibilities. You can even tie all the

The heat-retaining interior "trombe" wall of the
Lawrence home
*Credit:* Diana Vallera

systems together with a computer network that will monitor energy and
water use.

In their home, the Lawrences used an age-old construction tech-
nique to take advantage of the sun's heat. They designed the house
around a "trombe" wall. This attractive, passive-solar masonry structure
stores the sun's heat from south-facing windows in the winter months,
then releases it throughout the living space. Although a low-tech concept that has been in use for thousands of years, the element added
to the cost of the home and required the special building expertise
of their Chicago-based architect Tom Greene and their local builder
Rick McCanse. With the trombe wall and other energy-miser features,
McCanse estimates, "76 percent of the home's heat is self-supplied." The
trombe wall brilliantly manages to store and release heat without combustion, sparing the atmosphere carbon dioxide and the poison carbon
monoxide.

All of these features cost the Lawrences dearly. With copper gutters, extensive natural wood trim, and tight insulation, the cost of the

home was considerably higher than that of a tract home. The Lawrences paid a hefty $268.50 per square foot for the 4,000-square-foot house (including the large unfinished basement). Paying more for greener materials means more durability, though. The gutters and 24-gauge steel roof have a lifespan estimated at one hundred years. They also paid $37,100 for a wind turbine and $24,000 for solar panels to generate electricity, even though they didn't receive any tax subsidies to offset its cost. The total cost of the home, including $61,100 for energy systems and $151,800 in architectural fees, was $1.07 million.

The benefits are more than appreciated by the Lawrences. They not only show off the home as if it were a livable laboratory for green building, they've also been gradually restoring the oak savanna and upland prairie landscape to its original state from degraded pastureland. They've been removing invasive species such as leafy spurge and garlic mustard and planting native flowers and forbs such as phlox, yellow cone flowers, little bluestem grass, asters, and Jacob's ladder. "We wanted to live in nature," says Kathy Lawrence. "If we hadn't bought the land, a developer would have. This is the little piece we can help with."

As with the relationships between energy, ecology, and economy, there is a direct connection between the built environment, or anthroscape, and human health. Although concerned homeowners often focus on indoor air pollutants, abundant evidence suggests that the housing boom has triggered a wave of outdoor-pollution-related problems that negatively affect the majority of people living in urban areas.

With the expansion of the metroscape, the urban-suburban landscape, many of these ills have been amplified over the more than sixty years of the postwar building surge. Some of the most pressing health concerns are directly tied to greater mortality and morbidity rates (the growth of disease). Many of the declines in health conditions are directly attributable to unlimited suburban expansion.

## The Faux-Green Phenomenon

Not everyone involved in green building shares the Lawrences' overarching concern for the environment. Some of the homes offered under the green label are hardly green at all. To find an example of the faux-green phenomenon, you need go no further than the Orlando area in Florida. A necklace of toll roads and expressways links the major theme park areas. The city itself, which I visited only after more than a decade of traveling to the surrounding area, is a seeming afterthought to the entertainment enclaves of Kissimmee and other distractions on Interstate 4. Orlando is about a three-hour drive from the Fort Myers area. The route passes through some lovely coastal regions that are sparsely populated until you reach the Tampa–St. Petersburg area.

When I reach the entertainment capital of the Southeast, my first stop is the Gaylord Palms, a resort complex designed to remind you that you're in Florida even though you're under a gargantuan glass and steel dome. It's like going to Florida without ever going outside. Inside are a hotel, convention center, several shops and restaurants, and a meandering river landscaped with plants that can survive under the air-conditioned dome. There's a spa, a fake river, faux shotgun shacks, concrete palm trees galore, and real alligators that are trapped in the ersatz river. The Gaylord is yet another destination that could just as easily be in Buffalo, Omaha, or Peoria.

I'm staying at the Gaylord Palms because I'm attending conventions and conducting interviews. The Gaylord is one of those spurb destinations that's designed to keep you there. You can't walk anywhere because there are no sidewalks and busy highways surround the building. Disney World's entrance is within walking distance, although a phalanx of highway ramps prevents you from getting there alive. The odd feeling about the Gaylord is that it's somehow comforting to be among the fakery in the dome. It triggers some sort of biophilic (affinity for natural environments) response. The antithesis of the John Portman–designed hotels, with monster, soaring atriums and glass elevator columns, the Gaylord is the artificial environment's virtual triumph over the sweltering Florida weather. Without cheap energy, none of what the Gaylord symbolizes would be possible. If anything, in a dystopian sense, the dome reminds me of the eighteenth-century English philosopher Jeremy Bentham's prison building, Panopticon, which was originally designed to allow guards a 360-degree view of its wards.

Because the International Builders' Show is in town at the Orange County Convention Center, a short car trip from the Gaylord, this is one of the few Florida business trips for which I can muster modest enthusiasm. Threading my way up Interstate 4, I encounter the maddening traffic that plagues Orlando during the Disney season. There is not enough parking near the convention center, which looks like a row of modernized Wurlitzer juke boxes, so I park off-site and take a shuttle bus. No shuttle runs from the Gaylord.

After browsing the massive convention floor, I venture to an outside venue that is the green section of the show, which is a major event of the National Association of Home Builders, the trade association that sponsors the convention. I am first enticed by a modular home by Renaissance Home Builders, which is based in Addison, Alabama. The company was trying to build modestly priced products (under $200,000) for homeowners who lost their domiciles in the Hurricane Katrina debacle. I ask a representative how many of these homes the company is building, and he shrugs his shoulders, noting that there aren't enough building inspectors to even look at his homes, which can be trucked to the site and come with solar panels. Such is the state of disaster recovery in the Bush *fin de siècle*.

Another model, billed as the NextGen home, is marketed for its durability in hurricane-force winds and features a sturdy roof, shatter-proof glass, and tough walls. It, too, features solar panels, although they are downplayed in the presentation. Various producers of insulation and wall panels are hawking their energy-efficient attributes. Crowds stream in and out of the houses, which are literally sitting in the middle of a parking lot as if they were carnival sideshows.

For the first time in my decades of travel to Florida, I am going to see downtown Orlando. Its premier green home, a Broadway-quality attraction, is nowhere near the convention center, and you need special tickets to ride a bus to downtown. Billed as "the New American Home," the house was commissioned by the builders' association and built from scratch using local contractors and architects. It's a signature that the association has been promoting since 1984. On the bus, a video plays over and over extolling the virtues of a foam wall-insulation product being exhibited at the show. "More than $13 billion is lost every year through cracks in buildings," the narrator says, as if he's doing a World War II documentary.

Downtown Orlando's historic district is a pleasant surprise due to its reasonable size and genuine feel and its embrace of Lake Eola, which has a fountain in the middle of it and a path around its perimeter. This is not a disagreeable anthroscape (man-made/built environment). There is some comfort in the tight layout of the downtown, although there doesn't seem to be enough green space. With a view of the lake, the New American Home cuts a handsome profile at first. It's a whimsical blend of Arts and Crafts, Frank Lloyd Wright's Usonian, and modernist ideas. A three-story concrete house, the New American Home is designed to take the edge off the worst of Florida's weather and produce some energy to boot. Belted with three rings of green facade, the horizontal access of the house is offset by graceful, arched support beams that complement the other Craftsman-era homes in the city's historic district, which retains a delightful residue of charm from the period between 1905 and 1925. Prairie style meets contempo in an artful fusion of browns and greens that don't clash with the Spanish moss and live oaks. Canary Island palms front the brick street, which runs straight into the downtown high-rise district a few blocks away.

The 4,700-square-foot American home doesn't pretend to be an ersatz French suburban chateau. It strives for integration into the urban landscape with a retaining wall that separates it from the sidewalk, generous balconies, an "in-law" apartment over the garage, and a safe room for riding out a hurricane. The builders have tapped nearly every major manufacturer of building supplies, electronic gizmos, kitchen and bath fixtures, and appliances to put on a display of amenities. Attractive tour guides with stylish hair and frenetic, memorized deliveries usher small groups in and out of every single room, so the tour takes an hour and a half, including the time waiting outside.

When I ask the well-groomed guides whether they had any detailed information on wall insulation, window emissivity, or how many kilowatts the nearly invisible solar panels on the roof produce, they look at me as if I've asked about their personal hygiene. Instead of giving me answers, they regale me with a script on special amenities like the hideaway home theater and music systems from Bose, the HomeWorks lighting system from Lutron Electronics, and the Whirlpool Duet clothes washer-dryer, which has the "largest capacity of any residential frontload product available." The combination, in its sleek, stainless-steel cabinet, is Energy Star rated, of course, so there's some guilt assuaged in the laundry room at least.

The home is equipped with an estimable power plant. Producing a generous 10 kilowatts are twenty 2-by-4-foot photovoltaic panels, a 25-kilowatt standby generator to ease the occupants through storm-induced power outages, and three (count 'em) air-conditioning compressors to serve a pair of 17.8 SEER (seasonal energy efficiency ratio; that is, high efficiency) heat pumps and a 15 SEER gas and electric unit just for the third-level living space. Since all the air distribution is located in conditioned space, the designers claim a 58 percent whole-house energy savings. This is baffling to me since one heating-and-air-conditioning unit and fewer appliances would consume much less power. Attractive planters that allow water to drain into gutters largely hide the rooftop energy complex, which is ample enough to handle a small commercial building. So much for saving on the power bill. "How much power does this home consume when you have all of the electronics and appliances going?" I ask one of the young guides. "We don't exactly know," one of the chic young women snaps back.

Odd, urbane details like a wet bar in the narrow hallway bespeak of a Manhattan apartment instead of a modified bungalow in the middle of Florida. A spacious loft-like kitchen, dining room, and family room space with a broad terrace graces the third floor. It holds, you guessed it, all of the latest KitchenAid, Sub-Zero, and Wolf appliances.

I want to get away from this hour-long commercial and hang out on the patio, but I am ushered back downstairs as the next tour creeps up the metal stairway. The master bath is like a spa, only it could be in *your* home. The WaterHaven "custom shower tower" from Kohler on display in the master bath is like something out of a Fritz Lang movie, with four adjustable body sprays, two heads, and a handheld shower. The main bath even has a lovely glass waterfall as large as one of my old apartments in Chicago. So much for reduced water consumption. To their credit, though, the designers added a rainfall retention system that collects the water in a 7,000-gallon cistern underneath the garage floor; that water can be used for irrigating native plants in the dry winter months.

All told, the home, with the in-law apartment, was expected to sell for between $3 million and $4 million. It seemed like the appliances, fixtures, and amenities alone were worth at least $1 million. I walked next door to spy the remodeled bungalow called "the renewed American home," but bolted the tour after fifteen minutes. I just couldn't stand the product commercials anymore. As turkey buzzards soared overhead, I contemplated this latest manifestation of urban eco-chic. Could such a home—with all its gadgets sucking up electrons and indirectly pumping carbon dioxide into the air—be worthy of a "green" appellation? How could the tower of shower in the main bath actually conserve water in a state plagued with water woes?

Nothing about this palace of technology with its security monitors and flat-panel displays in nearly every room was remotely austere. Who is going to be able to afford this home? Certainly not someone pinching pennies by saving on energy bills or a forward-thinking young professional. If anything, the buyers will purchase it to induce "green envy" in their social sphere. How many homes have hallway bars *and* solar panels?

Twentieth-century sociologist and economist Thorstein Veblen, the man who coined the phrase "conspicuous consumption," would have clucked over this display of conspicuous *conservation*. Frank Lloyd Wright might have applauded it. The home is less about the sustainably harvested wood floors than it is about saying that you can *afford* to be green. As presented, the house seems a mere receptacle for a collection of energy-hungry appliances. This is a structure with a larger-than-average carbon footprint, but hey, it has a monster energy-efficient power and cooling system. Who cares about affordability when you have a great view of a lake in a big city and nobody will complain about looking at a bank of dorky solar panels? You have a huge water tank in your garage, and nobody can tell you when *not* to water your custom native landscaping. You'll even have reserve power to watch a Gators game when the next hurricane sweeps through the state. Could life be any hipper than this? Green is *good*.

Environmentalism is not only satisfying in a home setting, it's entertaining. In light of global warming, the cultural elite have taken up the green cause like the red, white, and blue medallions of French revolutionaries. At the center of this good will and a need to address global warming is the ironic attachment to a new form of consumerism—green homebuilding. Why shunt rainwater off to the sewer system when you can recycle it for your lush landscaping? Why not power those flat-panel displays in every room with solar-generated power? Still need a water-intensive Jacuzzi or shower tower? They can be fitted with low-flow faucets.

Like many of the homes in Florida in 2007 and 2008, the homebuilders' New American Home sat unsold on the market. Initially listed at $3.1 million, the price was reduced to $2.8 million before builder Carmen Dominguez took it off the market and decided to use it as her office until the market improved. Even the decked-out, greened-up, earth-toned show palace of American builders couldn't find a buyer.

CHAPTER 7

# Building Smarter

THE HARSH STREET NOISE and rumbling Berkeley city bus that stops just a few feet from us doesn't distract Californian Michelle Kaufmann from her exuberant message and lively gesticulation as we sit talking in a cafe. Although she doesn't know Victor Zaderej or the Lawrences, she has picked up where they left off in revitalizing, reinventing, and rebuilding the American home—in a factory. She may become to home-building what Henry Ford was to automaking.

If she succeeds where so many have failed, Kaufmann will transform the homebuilding industry worldwide. Her work will also make homes affordable in places where land prices have made building the best-possible structure cost-prohibitive for most middle-income home buyers. Her homes are manufactured, yet they defy the image of a factory-built home. They are highly energy efficient, use recycled and sustainable materials, conserve water, produce power, and can be shipped out and assembled on-site onto a permanent foundation. You wouldn't find one of her homes in a trailer park.

With the charisma of a politician and dazzling green eyes that dance with the ideas of a dynamic inner life, Kaufmann is the prophetess of what homebuilding can become. Innovation-rich Berkeley is the per-fect setting to engage Kaufmann, who is carrying her purse-sized dog Peekay along as she orders a sandwich. It was the insane price of real estate that originally drove Michelle and her husband Kevin to consider alternatives to the standard, stick-built homes. "The options available to me were $600,000 teardowns—which we could almost afford but then couldn't once we tore the building down—or developer subdivision mini-McMansions," she says, sipping her water quickly. "So we decided to build something for ourselves. We found some land and started building our simple, sustainable home."

With Kevin acting as a contractor, Kaufmann searched for the kind of green materials that would do the least amount of harm to old-growth forests, the Amazon, and other imperiled areas. That led her to the idea of mass-producing such a home in a modular fashion, which spawned her Glidehouse concept. Although their site-built home took eleven months longer to build than she had projected, the new modular design could be built in four months, which is roughly two months less than it would take for an average-sized stick-built home. With refinements in her factory designs and construction, the construction time will continue to shorten, although the time for a given house will depend on the amount of customization.

Architects and builders from Frank Lloyd Wright to mainstream home manufacturers have tried to sell factory-built homes in middle-class suburbia and failed on a large scale. The perception has always been that these kinds of homes have been flimsy, tornado-attracting tuna cans, and the quality wasn't worthy of buyers willing to spend more than $200,000 for a home. Kaufmann, who has a master's degree in architecture from Princeton, worked as an associate with world-renowned architect Frank Gehry for five years, designing museum exhibits. Kaufmann's homes are deceptively simple because they're trucked onto a site and assembled by crane. They come in modules, boxes that can be attached to each other with relatively little labor in a fraction of the time it would take to construct a stick-built house.

## Inside the Smart Home

Several months after our first conversation, I met Kaufmann again as she was putting her "Smart Home" in place at the Museum of Science and Industry in Chicago. Five modules were being removed from flatbeds and lifted onto a foundation in the courtyard of the museum, nestled between the Henry Crown Space Center and the oldest part of the complex, which dates to the World's Columbian Exposition of 1893. "Setting" the house took only a few hours, although four months of factory assembly preceded the event.

Michelle Kaufmann's "Smart Home" at the Museum of Science and Industry in Chicago
*Credit:* John Swain Photography

The fact that her 2,500-square-foot home had become an exhibit in the western hemisphere's largest science and technology museum is a nod to how innovative Kaufmann's design is; it has become the show-piece home of the future that world's fairs *used to* promote, although most of the technology employed to build it is not particularly cutting edge. Her revolutionary mkSolaire museum home is on hallowed ground. A Frank Lloyd Wright Usonian home sat in the same courtyard in 1989. Wright had designed a Usonian automatic home (employing simple construction) but never built it. Like Kaufmann's home, the Wright design featured modular sections, but the builders decided to modify the walls into load-bearing panels consisting of a polystyrene core, wafer board, and a cement-like coating. Originally designed to be assembled by the future homeowners themselves, this model was to be Wright's home for the masses. It was projected to cost from $10,000 to $20,000 in the 1950s. Builders in the '80s assembled the 1,800-square-foot home for about $300,000, which was pricey for that time.

Like Wright, Kaufmann uses preassembled panels that are well insulated and designed to eliminate waste and reduce labor costs. The home's exterior is clad with cement board and Ipe, a Brazilian wood grown in sustainable forests. The idea of building a home from scratch, using two-by-fours and thousands of nails over the better part of a year, is anathema to her. "Automation and technology is in every other industry," she says with repugnance. "The construction industry, in contrast, is antiquated, broken, wasteful, and time-consuming. It's like asking someone to build a car in a driveway. There's 50 to 75 percent less waste when you build a home in a factory."

The waste involved in building a stick-built home can amount to several tons, depending on the size of the home. A 2,000-square-foot single-family home, about five hundred feet under the national average for new American homes, consumes about 14,000 board feet of framing lumber, 11,000 square feet of sheathing, and 17 tons of concrete. Laid end to end, the trail of lumber for a 3,000-square-foot home would be four miles long. Upgrading to 5,000 square feet triples the amount of materials needed. As the size of new homes has increased—even as household size has dropped from about four family members in 1940 to fewer than three in the twenty-first century—so has the construction waste. It costs energy to ship, remove, and bury all of that waste. The construction of one 2,500-square-foot home produces the equivalent of thirty-six metric tons of carbon dioxide.

The language Kaufmann uses to describe how her homes are built reflects a paradigm shift in the thinking about homebuilding. Her houses are assembled on site with cranes and "set up" rather than constructed. Once in place, the modules are *buttoned up* as opposed to being finished. All of the modules come complete with walls already wired, plumbed, and set up for a high-efficiency heating system. Miniducts roughly the size of a man's fist shoot air through the house at high velocity. The speed of the air makes the home feel cooler in summer, and radiant floor heating makes it comfortable underfoot in the winter. The design employs passive-solar thermal retention and green roofs that not only allow you to grow things on them but also save rainwater for irrigation. The wood used in the handsome exterior is sustainably harvested and certified by the Forest Stewardship Council.

Echoing Wright's organic architecture mantra, Kaufmann wants her clients to "live cleanly and lightly in a home that is in harmony with its surroundings." Her Glidehouse was on display at the National Building Museum in Washington and her mkSolaire and Sunset Breezehouse have been profiled in numerous magazines. Kaufmann captures the spirit of democratic architecture when she launches into how important pricing is to her. Her focus on bringing the cost per unit down while providing a quality product reminded me of the breakthroughs of the second industrial revolution in the late nineteenth and early twentieth centuries. If she can mass-produce her green homes at a low cost, it would be a world-changing breakthrough on a par with the breakthroughs of Ford and Edison.

## The Energy-Intensive Home and How It Started

The Chicago Museum of Science and Industry site bears a powerful historical pedigree that has shaped the modern metropolis where some 21 million visitors saw a comprehensive vision of the future during the World's Columbian Exposition in 1893. What a scene of contrasts! The gleaming White City with its combination of beaux arts facades, electric trolleys, a midway with a giant Ferris wheel, and thousands of items most Americans had never seen on such a scale: electric light bulbs and motors.

The fair, created by the joint talents of Daniel Hudson Burnham and Frederick Law Olmsted, was hosted by Chicago, which, at the time, was the fastest-growing city on earth, although it was still mired in the nineteenth-century milieu. Thousands of saloons served up their potables because the drinking water from the lake was constantly tainted with the offal of slaughterhouses and raw sewage. Yet the theme of the fair was engineering the new age and how technology would make the twentieth century an electrified utopia.

In the fair's Westinghouse pavilion, the electrical genius Nikola Tesla did his own bizarre sideshow to demonstrate running a million volts through his lanky frame. It helped immensely that he was wearing rubber boots during his show. After the fair, nearly every major city would see the power of his idea—alternating current—and wire their towns using his technology, the operating system of the twentieth century. Town fathers originally wanted the electricity to illuminate their streets and power electric trolleys. The latter would eliminate horse-drawn trolleys, which resulted in millions of tons of manure, yet another source of disease.

Seeing the light of the future at the fair was Samuel Insull, a bulldog of a businessman who cashed in his General Electric (GE) stock after virtually starting and managing the company as its first chief executive (although he never had that title) for Thomas Edison in New York. Insull, whose life I detailed in my book *Merchant of Power,* saw the potential to not only light the streets of entire cities but also give their citizenries electric lights, irons, vacuum cleaners, refrigerators, and twenty-four-hour electric service. His Chicago Edison Company and subsequent acquisitions created the modern electrical grid and electrified offices, factories, and homes.

Insull began his empire by consolidating tiny Chicago Edison with other small generating companies. At the time, Chicago Edison had one building on Adams Street, which did triple duty as its headquarters, dynamo room, and coal bin. Having accepted the Chicago job for $12,000—a drastic pay cut compared to the $36,000 he was making at GE—he knew that electrical rates did not compete with gas rates when he arrived in the Windy City. In fact, electric power at the time cost 50 percent more than the dim, dangerous gas used to illuminate most homes and buildings. He then proceeded to cut electrical rates to twenty cents a kilowatt-hour and kept on cutting until he reached two and a half cents per kilowatt-hour in 1909 (the average U.S. cost was about eight cents an hour in 2008).

The aggressive economics Insull employed worked as he gave away flatirons, cut deals to wire homes and factories, and unleashed his powerful marketing machine whose credo was "early to bed, early to rise, advertise, advertise, advertise!" What the balloon frame was to homebuilding, Insull's electrical pricing and generation system was to mass electrification. In 1892, his company had five thousand customers; fourteen years later, he had two hundred thousand. Along the way Insull brought in power meters, created state utility commissions, built the Chicago Civic Opera House, and ended up serving some six thousand communities across the country. The energy-intensive home, office, and factory were largely Insull's brainchild.

Although Insull saw the fair as a business opportunity, Olmsted, the godfather of modern landscape architecture and urban planning, had his feet firmly planted in the "city beautiful" philosophy of making cities habitable. Having designed Jackson Park, New York's Central Park, and the first planned suburb, Riverside (only a few miles from the Chicago fair site), Olmsted wanted the exposition to reflect what modern life could look like. Nature could coexist with the electron in every community. His parks, planned with his partner Calvert Vaux, were graced by abundant meadows, gentle ponds, and curving promenades.

Riverside, built a few years after the Civil War, reflected the philosophy that a community outside the city could be a healthful and renewing place. Generous parks and river vistas graced the small town, which hit hard times in the aftermath of the Chicago fire in 1871 and a recession in the early 1890s. As such, it was one of the first master-planned, transit-oriented developments, a concept that sorely needs revisiting today as every metropolitan area grapples with traffic and sprawl.

Chicago was at the vanguard of urban growth and architecture in the three decades following the great fire of 1871. In the decade prior to the fair, the skyscraper was born in the city. The production of steel beams through the Bessemer process made taller buildings possible. Before then, the limit on buildings supported by masonry walls was from ten to sixteen stories. Soon steel skeletons and new electric elevators enabled architects to design behemoths that soared much higher. A leading architectural firm captained by Louis Sullivan and Dankmar Adler built the Auditorium Building, which was a hotel, opera house, and office building. It stood as a colossus in 1893; the tallest building in the world at the time, with its charming Tuscan-like tower and hulking stone presence lording over Congress and Michigan. One of the young men who worked on the tower with Sullivan was his chief assistant Frank Lloyd Wright.

Needing more income to support his wife and six children in Oak Park, the former apprentice was to break off on his own in the year of the 1893 fair, much to the consternation of his *lieber meister,* Sullivan. Working in Sullivan's firm, Wright did some of the drawings and designs that employed Sullivan's idea of organic ornament. Filigrees of leaves and trees adorn Sullivan buildings, as if they've sprung out of a meadow or forest. Wright took Sullivan's natural sensibilities further. He wanted homes and buildings to harmonize with the earth and not just depict it.

Burnham saw Wright's talent and wanted to lure him away from Sullivan, so he made a generous offer to Wright, demeaning his brilliant mentor Sullivan as a "great decorator." Burnham promised to pay for Wright's education at the School of Beaux Arts in Paris plus two additional years of study in Rome if he would join his firm Burnham and Root upon his graduation. Wright was stunned. "It was more than merely generous," Wright later said of the proposal. "It was splendid. But I was frightened. I sat embarrassed not knowing what to say." Eventually

Wright did find the words to refuse the powerful sway of Burnham's personality.

Wright was the bridge between the organic splendors of Sullivan and the neoclassical sensibilities of Burnham, who would design classic buildings, such as New York's Flatiron, and later develop Chicago's landmark city plan of 1909. Sometime around 1893, the collective genius of Burnham, Sullivan, Wright, and Insull managed to coalesce. Perhaps they met at Jane Addams's Hull House in the Near West Side, where there was an active arts and crafts society and iconoclasts like Wright were invited to share their ideas.

I like to believe that these great minds spiritually met in one place: the Ho-o-Den Temple on Wooded Island in the lagoon created by Olmsted behind the fair's Arts Building, now the Museum of Science and Industry. It would have been a quiet, sylvan refuge in the middle of the bustle of the exposition. Inspired by the philosophy of the temple—a short walk from Kaufmann's Smart Home—Wright created an American style of organic architecture that flouted convention and embraced natural design at every turn. The Prairie School of Architecture would emerge a few years later. Maybe Insull sold Wright on wiring his new homes with built-in electric fixtures—innovations artfully on display nearby in Wright's revolutionary Robie House, which still sits sphinx-like across from the University of Chicago Booth School of Business. A few blocks away is the birthplace of nuclear power and the home of Barack Obama.

Within twenty years of the fair, Insull would marry the coal-burning steam turbine with a dynamo to create the first large-scale turbogenerator at his Fisk Street Station, which is still running a few miles north of the museum. This quantum leap in technology meant that entire cities could be powered. Every street, office, and home could have clean, safe electric lights. Factories could have motors that didn't need inefficient pulleys powered by noisy steam engines. Housewives could throw away those nasty flatirons that constantly burned them. Offices could keep their workers longer and make them more productive.

The modern age may have been imagined by Burnham, but it was engineered and marketed by Insull, whose business plan was to make profits by selling more electrons. His coal-fired technology is still the dominant method of electricity generation in the world today, largely because coal is so abundant and cheap relative to other fuel sources. To this day, following Insull's "gospel of consumption," the modern home and metropolis become ever more energy intensive with each passing year as Americans plug in an endless array of new power-hungry appliances.

## The American Dream Updated

The influential innovation of the Chicago fair and the people who were inspired by it can be seen in myriad subtle details in the Kaufmann home. Whereas Insull sought to boost power consumption in every room, Kaufmann seeks to conserve it, even though Commonwealth Edison, the local company founded by Insull, was one of the sponsors of the exhibit.

Kaufmann's home integrates nature, form, and function. Aesthetically, it pays homage to Wright's Fallingwater masterpiece in Pennsylvania with its cantilevered balcony and harmonic interplay among cubist forms. She uses materials in a much more organic way than Wright did with his masterpiece. The dark wood siding blends in better with a lushly wooded site (there's a small grove of mature burr oaks in the museum courtyard that was there in Olmsted's day), and the tower connecting the two stories permits the growth of vines to mask its relatively gray starkness. Since the home has a system to retain rainwater, all of the greenery on the roof (there are three decks) and the surrounding landscaping are essentially self-watering in drier months.

The Smart Home has a utilitarian elegance that is not the least bit pretentious. There's not a trace of mock–French chateau, English-cottage, or Gothic ornament. This is a house borne of geometry and purpose. It's abstract yet organic, not fighting with the site as do so many modern homes. When I remark to Kaufmann that her ideas remind me of Wright's Usonian homes, which he hoped to mass-produce with Wisconsin builder Marshall Erdman, she is flattered.

In his designs, Wright took the sacred covenant that Victorians had with home making and transformed it into an open, democratic unity with nature. He wanted his buildings to harmonize with their surroundings. Long eaves and cantilevered porches mimicked the horizontal grace of Midwestern grasslands. Even his windows incorporated abstractions of natural shapes such as wheat or hollyhocks.

The core of a Wright home was typically the hearth, the "sanctum sanctorum" for the family. His most-celebrated designs placed a great importance on the fireplace as a spiritual symbol. Inventing the term *Usonian*, a blending of a Samuel Butler phrase for utopia and the United States, Wright exemplified his idea of organic form and function in his Usonian homes. Even his Wisconsin home, Taliesin, was "of" the hill rather than merely on top of it. His masterpiece Fallingwater, near Bear Run, Pennsylvania, emerges over a waterfall as if nature intended it to be built there.

The owners of the Pope-Leighey House, another of Wright's Usonian models, said their home "spoke to the spirit." But in his voluminous writings, one powerful sentiment that moved Wright came from Jefferson. He called his organic approach "the architecture of democracy." It didn't mean that every structure would be equal or that every man would be able to afford one of his designs; most of his custom homes were built for the well-heeled. Wright placed the ego at the middle of his buildings—more often than not *his*—to the frequent delight and frustration of his clients. Homes for Wright often became personal statements and less sacred enclaves. As architectural historian Jonathan Hale puts it, "In Wright's architecture of democracy, you are at the center; you are *always* at the center. It is the essence of democracy that everyone is at the center."

You can see the egocentric, democratic ethic almost every time you walk into a custom home. Observe the expansive atrium as you enter. Does this space serve any other useful purpose than to say, "I can afford square footage that is nothing but air designed to make visitors gasp?"

Although Wright didn't care much for rooms that were mostly filled with air—he could create uniquely intimate interiors—he echoed Jefferson again when he designed his Broadacre City in the early 1930s (see Chapter 11). Along with Jefferson, Wright was an influential synthesizer of ideas into plastic form: Like Jefferson, he injected his philosophy into his sites and buildings.

Smart Homes are rebellious—a testament to the truth that most houses are outdated, expensive, and wasteful. Although home buyers will always be willing to pay more for luxury features, house construction can follow the rules of mass production. If you can build them in factories as modular units, their overall costs will drop and more people will be able to afford them. The market is small for million-dollar homes with solar panels installed as a status symbol, but the market for

$250,000, green modular homes is huge. The American dream can be healthy, energy efficient, and affordable.

If green building is to succeed at all, modular homes have to be priced and delivered with the least amount of effort on the part of the homebuyer. Does that mean a return to the "kit" bungalow of the Sears Craftsman homes of the early twentieth century? In a sense yes, except the delivered product would interact with the local environment to produce and retain energy and resources and the modules could be assembled by professionals on-site. That's the next step in making green homes accessible to the mass market.

## The Beauty of Nothing Wasted

Like Wright, Kaufmann focuses on simplicity and elegance, yet she also concentrates on cost. It's hard to fathom why it took so long—Wright's mass production venture essentially failed in the 1950s—but Kaufmann is clearly on to an idea whose time has come. She built her first Glidehouse for $363,950, which was hardly a bargain at $233 a square foot—excluding the cost of the land. The average price per square foot for new American stick-built homes was about $92 in 2008. (Add another $20 for the additional costs of building in the Western states.)

The overall price for Kaufmann's home was a steal for the Bay Area, where land, labor, and materials costs are typically way above the national average. By 2007, she was able to improve on earlier costs with her factory-built Glidehouse, priced at $224,000 plus $34,500 for shipping and $32,000 for additional "button-up" work. That brought the package price down to $182 a square foot. That's still no extraordinary value in the Midwest or South, but it's eminently affordable by California or East Coast standards.

As equipped, the museum house would cost about $450,000 to $500,000, which still doesn't include the price of land, landscaping, or furnishing expenses. Again, it's certainly not a great value and it's well above the average for Midwestern homes, but not overpriced for an upscale high-performance home. Kaufmann hopes to bring down the price if the homes are mass-produced. "There are easily packaged solutions," she says. "Our goal is ten thousand modular homes in the next decade. We want to design for disassembly, outsource cores like bathrooms and kitchens that have on-demand water and solar heat.

We can get the cost down to $140 to $150 a square foot plus the site cost [land and preparation]."

By assembling in a factory, Kaufmann conquers some of the major environmental pitfalls of twentieth-century homebuilding. Waste is reduced dramatically since the house is 90 percent complete when it arrives on-site. Leftover materials can be kept at the factory for reuse. The finished product is ready in six weeks versus six months, meaning the energy and labor consumed in building it are reduced. Since the house is built indoors and assembled on-site, there are few, if any, weather-related delays. All American Homes, a subsidiary of the recreational vehicle maker Coachmen Industries, assembled the museum home in a factory in Decatur, Indiana, in three weeks. In a controlled environment, the modules can be fabricated in three weeks, which means that total (factory versus on-site) construction time is 60 percent faster than that for stick-built homes.

Waste is pared down in the Kaufmann model because all of the lumber is precision cut and sawdust is recycled to heat the factory. Even drywall scrap is recycled to local farms. All told, the factory process knocks an estimated eleven months off the total time needed to build a stick-built home, resulting in a $51-per-square-foot labor savings. By talking about adding additional value to the process through supply-chain optimization, large-scale factory production, and strategic partner management, Kaufmann sounds more like a manufacturer than an architect, all in a quest to lower prices while enhancing quality. Back in the real world of labor unions, custom building, and entrenched practices, she reflects on the causes of the housing bubble.

"My thesis is that Americans were pushed beyond their economic limits simply because housing had become unaffordable. Then the market responded to this demand. That being said, I think that the current financial quandary that many Americans find themselves in has a lot to do with a lifestyle based on consumption of quantity over quality. Conventional real estate and stick-built homes are often sold on the premise that bigger is better. Square footage for square footage's sake. The sheer quantity of poorly designed and rarely used rooms does not add to the quality of enjoyment of a person's life. Rather, it translates into higher mortgage, utility, maintenance, and tax payments."

The "smartness" of the Kaufmann home comes in the form of the energy-monitoring system. Homeowners can directly gauge how much energy they use and where, directing heating and cooling to rooms they occupy. This is called "cybernetic ecology," whereby a computer can monitor, control, and reduce energy and resource use. "Some one-third of heating is wasted on spaces you don't inhabit," Kaufmann has found. A low-tech feature that goes back millennia is a tower that acts as a chimney, pulling hot air up and out during warm days. Fresh air is brought in through a filtering system and sent through two-inch-wide, high-velocity flexible tubes, which reduces the need for (and cost of) sheet-metal ducting. Hot water is provided by an on-demand heater, which is also energy efficient and takes up less space than the missile-shaped water heaters with huge tanks and constantly heated reservoirs.

Optional photovoltaic film provides a modest 2.5 kilowatts of power. The modular walls mean the home is extremely well-sealed. Triple-pane windows dramatically reduce heat loss. Water from washing can be recycled in a "gray water" system, although Chicago city ordinances didn't permit it as of 2008.

The exteriors are low-maintenance, durable, and designed to be stronger than those of conventional homes. The interiors contain bamboo or recycled glass flooring, recycled paper countertops, low-energy lighting, recycled glass tile, water-saving toilets and fixtures, tankless water heaters, and dual-flush toilets. The indoor surfaces are coated with no-VOC paints, and there's no formaldehyde in the cabinetry. The walls are insulated with Icynene spray-in foam, with every wood-to-wood joint caulked for additional tightness. Windows are situated to absorb the proper amount of solar radiation and the roofs sloped for solar panels, although these appliances are additional purchases.

Kaufmann still faces enormous obstacles such as inbred biases against manufactured housing, which is wrongly lumped together with shoddy trailer parks. Building codes will have to be rewritten to accommodate modular construction and its different yet higher standards. She needs to work with the building trades so they don't start picketing her labor-saving techniques such as cutting construction waste and labor by 50 percent to 75 percent. Then there's the tremendous amount of education that needs to be done with the home buyers, who still are fixated on customizing their homes with granite countertops rather than choosing appliances that produce power and lower operating costs. There is a huge wall to climb on all of these issues, yet she's undaunted and clings to her vision. "Just look at the cell phone. Now more is expected out of less. You can customize it. It's starting to shift—you can customize a modular home in your own way."

Others have followed Kaufmann's lead. LivingHomes, also based in California, was selling modular green homes starting at $265 per square foot, excluding land costs. The company said it hopes to bring that down to $155 per square foot. Although modular building is certainly not displacing stick-built building in most areas, it is catching on as builders seek new ways to market affordable homes. Companies such as Marmol Radziner Prefab, StalwartBuilt Homes, Innova Homes, Wardcraft Homes, and Ritz-Craft are featuring everything from recycled steel frames to solar water heating systems. Although the sales volumes of these companies are small relative to mainstream builders like Lennar Corp., these homes' appeal is growing as their prices and green features gain wider acceptance.

## Solar, Sexy, and Expensive

Can a home be even more energy conscious than Kaufmann's modular designs? Adding more solar panels and wind and geothermal appliances makes it possible to sell power back to the utility company on certain days, ushering in the era of the "zero-energy" home.

Just south of Berkeley, I traveled through a tunnel to Danville, California, one of those idyllic places where everything looks like it just came out of a Restoration Hardware catalog and is the location for another Steven Spielberg movie. In Danville, I visited Lennar's Milano development, where the new Mediterranean-style homes going up in this dry, verdant valley east of San Francisco will have solar panels, and were a portion of the 375 homes Lennar planned to build in the Bay Area. The homes, which have Internet connections that tell the sprinkler system when to go on, range in size from 3,000 to about 4,000 square feet, so they don't qualify as pure McMansions. The prices in the Milano development ranged from $1 million to $1.2 million in late 2008.

Solar homes in California are supported by state and local programs, which are creating a market for energy-producing houses. By late 2008, almost five thousand home solar systems had been installed in the Golden State, according to the California Energy Commission.

The million-dollar-plus home I toured was a 3,800-square-foot, two-story house with five bedrooms, four and a half baths, an office, a technology area, and a two-car garage in Milano. The house also included a security system, an intercom, high-speed Internet, a home theater, energy-efficient windows, and high-efficiency air conditioning.

Although most Americans can't afford this kind of home, it's not extravagant for the Bay Area, which features some of the priciest real estate in the country. All of the latest doodads are part of the package, ranging from a touch panel display of all of the networked systems in the home to a Web-based irrigation system that will check the weather and turn on the water when needed.

With the average U.S. family's household energy bill at almost $4,000 a year in 2008—the price of natural gas alone rose 48 percent between 2006 and 2008—reducing that monthly electric, gas, or oil bill is a top priority in millions of households. But is it worth a huge premium to buy green homes? It may be, if energy prices keep rising, as many analysts predict.

No matter how much energy they save, million-dollar solar homes are not going to revitalize the U.S. home market, not even in California. For a clue to how homes could become more energy conscious and still remain somewhat affordable, I looked at the Sacramento area, where the local utility supports green homebuilding and prices are much lower than in the Bay Area. Premier Homes of Roseville, based in an area where summer heat often exceeds 100 degrees, sold zero-energy homes equipped with solar panels, tankless water heaters, and additional insulation.

Although the prices of the houses ranged from $250,000 to $450,000—from $40,000 to $90,000 higher than similar houses in the area—they were selling in a slack market because they could offer utility bills that the builder claims are 60 percent lower than those of conventional homes. The builder tells buyers they can recoup the additional money spent on their "ProEnergy" homes with lower power bills. As with all U.S. builders employing energy-producing technology, Premier customers also benefited from a $2,000 federal tax credit for solar appliances and numerous incentives from the Sacramento Municipal Utility District, the public electric company. In an area in which $500 monthly summer electrical bills are common, the chance for saving on power bills was attracting home buyers in a lackluster market.

## The Green-Marketing Muddle

Nearly every home can be designed as smartly on the energy and health fronts as the Kaufmann or Lennar houses, but few are because household energy has historically been so cheap. Yet with energy bills becoming unaffordable for lower- and middle-income households, green homes shouldn't be custom built, which can cost homeowners up to $600 a square foot. A geothermal heating system can cost from $10,000 to $20,000 alone. Custom green building also doesn't solve the larger problem of making every home greener and reducing homeowners' expenses or carbon footprints.

Then there's the bugaboo of economic sustainability. Only a handful of homeowners have been willing to pay for green features, even though they will reduce ownership costs over time. The vast majority of U.S. homes continue to be built with the unhealthy, energy-intensive, nineteenth-century stick-built technology. During an era of high energy costs, this is an ongoing economic impairment that will extend beyond the housing bust.

Still, on a large scale, costs for green homebuilding can and will drop. Custom homes can be templates for entire new subdivisions and for remodeling or rebuilding inner suburbs. The promise of modular housing is that an entire structure can be created with precision engineering in a factory, reducing costs even more. There is so much that green building promises, yet that can't be delivered until the industry can realize and communicate cost savings to their customers. Countertops made of recycled materials are desirable and make for attractive pictures in shelter magazines, but they won't save homeowners a nickel in energy costs.

With millions of homeowners spending thousands every year for utility bills, the economic benefits of green homes need to be marketed as a primary value-added feature. Stickers need to be attached to property listings that detail specific energy-cost estimates similar to mileage stickers on cars or energy-consumption labels on appliances. Homes in total consume far more energy than washers, dryers, and refrigerators combined, yet long-term energy costs are not required to be disclosed by real estate agents. Say a home costs $2,500 a year in utility bills, which is entirely plausible for a 3,000-square-foot-plus single-family home. That's $50,000 over twenty years, or the price of one year at a top-tier Ivy League school. And this is not an expense that's constant like a fixed-rate mortgage. It can soar if a winter is unusually cold or a summer extremely hot. If electricity, as predicted, becomes morse expensive due to carbon taxes or infrastructure costs, the cost of running a home will also increase. Homeowners also have no control over utility rates, which have been on a long-term ascent.

## Subsidies Needed

Despite the sexiness of having the sun partially power your home, the economics of home solar power isn't favorable for most homeowners without huge, California-scale government subsidies. And due to public misconceptions, it may take years for green, modular building to take off on a large enough scale to put a dent in housing prices.

Almost no mainstream builders are set up to build and sell modular units. And they certainly are loath to build smaller, less profitable production homes, in which the profit is much tighter than the "shoot-the-moon, upgrade like crazy, and roll it into a 30-year mortgage" models. But green homes don't need to be elaborate to save on energy and construction costs. As Americans age and families get smaller, downsizing is becoming a viable marketing concept. The inescapable truth is that for the homeownership rate to rise or remain steady, the cost of building a home will have to drop dramatically to accommodate more buyers who are pinched by inflation, stagnant wages, loss of benefits, and the fraying of the social contract.

Then there's a factor that builders have no power over: No matter how energy efficient a home is, a builder can't do anything to reduce the cost of land, which is a hostage to supply, demand, building restrictions, public perception, the quality of local amenities, the tax base, and school districts. Builders can and will build entire subdivisions of energy-stingy power-producing homes, yet they will be supremely hypocritical if they are constructing the same old spurb that requires huge fossil-fuel consumption just to get there and back. Two fundamental changes that could spur green homebuilding would be incentives for utilities to reduce power consumption (that is, for customers to conserve more) and carbon taxes on structures that consume above-average energy resources.

Until energy saving is institutionalized into the tax and building codes, entire communities will need to be redesigned to avoid the cul-de-sac syndrome, the economic sickness that has plagued America for decades. To understand how that problem could be overcome, I traveled back to a seminal place of my youth: Park Forest, Illinois, one of the most comprehensively planned model postwar suburbs.

# CHAPTER 8

# The Near Death of a Suburb

I CAN STILL PICTURE the way it looked as I rode in on my bike. If there is such as thing as a schoolboy crush on a place, the Park Forest Plaza always got my juices flowing. It was the first destination I could pedal to in my preadolescent independence. An entire community had been built around the prototypical outdoor shopping center, the nexus of the brave, new postwar building boom in south suburban Chicago. It's a blissful image because Park Forest *seemed* perfect to me. It was so fresh, modern, and exciting.

A tricornered clock tower with minimalist dots for numbers was its most noticeable landmark. Sears, Roebuck anchored one corner, symbolizing the middle-class America that still did things for itself with plenty of tools, Levis, and car batteries. We went to Sears for underwear, car tires and batteries, Craftsman power tools, and hooded sweatshirts. This was the pre–Kmart, pre–hedge fund Sears, at its zenith the world's largest retailer. It had its own 50,000-watt radio station for a time in Chicago—WLS-AM, which stood for the "world's largest store." The retailer was headquartered in the world's largest building in downtown Chicago before its suburban executives moved it out to a soulless office park in the northwest suburbs. Its Christmas catalog was as thick as a Manhattan phone directory.

In another corner of the Plaza, Marshall Field's, with its patrician green and white awnings, attracted the upwardly mobile set. These shoppers wanted something infinitely more posh than Sears. They were the social climbers. This was the store where brides registered and where you bought fine china and could find a decent suit. My mom had a job

111

there working at the candy counter before it closed, one of her favorite jobs. Goldblatt's, the scrappy, bargain-basement godfather of Wal-Mart Stores, occupied a darker corner of the plaza. That's where you went to buy socks. Dollar days were advertised relentlessly in crass newspaper flyers. Whereas Field's had elegance and class, Goldblatt's was one step up from a souk.

The plaza had its own movie palace, which would show art films by directors ranging from Ingmar Bergman to Akira Kurosawa. Fannie May sold bonbons. Sports and Hobbies was the prototypical guy's store where I could buy rocket and chemistry supplies. A tiny locally owned bookstore was a compact version of today's megastores. They didn't serve cappuccino, but owner Harold Maeyama would personally recommend books if you asked.

I grew up in the next town over, Matteson, which was little more than a railroad stop when I was there in my preteens (it has since eclipsed Park Forest in population and economic clout). Our first library was in a storefront no wider than a Chevy Biscayne. When it expanded, it moved to a slightly larger storefront. That was pathetic compared to the Prairie-style palace Park Forest built for its books, which even housed the plucky Illinois Theatre Company in its basement (until it moved to the plaza decades later). As a lover of literature, my mother brought us to every library she could, but Park Forest's temple of knowledge was always a treat. There was even a pool complex called the Aqua Center next door, our paradise during the blistering Midwestern summers.

In the Park Forest library, you would find people like Joan Larsen, a resident since 1952 and a believer in the mission of Park Forest since its inception. Like many of her generation, Joan was an early builder of the civic bulwark that kept the town vibrant for decades and was a member of a number of associations, including the library board and United Way. The signs for these countless civic groups dotted the town, like too many medals on the chest of an old admiral.

Park Forest, a much-maligned model for William Whyte's classic *The Organization Man*, was a well-known breeding ground for corporate executives, scientists, and other professionals who worked downtown or within twenty miles of the model suburb. Joan's husband Paul (they first rented a townhouse in the village in 1955) worked at the Amoco Whiting Refinery, then at Standard Oil of Indiana (since absorbed into BP). In the 1950s and 1960s, it wasn't unusual to have a CEO or PhD living next to an accountant or teacher. It was a grand experiment in the broad-based middle-class society, where America seemed to be starting all over in 1946, thriving because of the GI bill and veterans' home-buying benefits. Abandoning dreary urban apartments, first-home buyers in Park Forest could have a place all their own—all 640 square feet of it. There couldn't have been a more progressive American town, reveling in its novelty and social cohesion.

## Creating a Model Community

Park Forest was everything Chicago was not. A tiny industrial park was neatly tucked into a quiet district next to Matteson. No smokestack industries here. More than twenty parks gave many residents a view of open space. The small schools were mostly within walking distance. Residents could rent cheaply, then upgrade to a "Futura" dream home, built on a slab (since the water table was so high), which came complete with carport and natural-gas appliances. It was upscale, affordable, clean, new, and nearly all white. "It was beautiful and safe to walk in," Larsen recalls of her early years in the suburb. "I was twenty-one years old when I moved in to one of the rental units and paid $95 per month. All of my neighbors were college grads and most were under twenty-five. We didn't lock our doors. We walked our babies to the plaza."

Like her neighbors, Larsen got involved in several of the dozens of civic organizations such as the League of Women Voters. In 1963, she and her husband moved into their own home, where they raised their family. Starting in 1952, Park Forest began building starter homes to meet the needs of veterans who wanted to start families. Developers Philip Klutznick and Nathan Manilow supplied Park Foresters with three-bedroom brick ranches starting at $13,200, although you could buy a tract home for as little as $11,000.

For an attached carport with "storage wall," the starting price was $14,800. Toward the end of the decade, Cape Cods came on the market for $17,000, followed by split-levels for $20,000. A "choice location overlooking a forest preserve or school recreation area" would cost $3,000 extra.

More than three thousand rental units were built from 1948 through 1950, with the idea that buyers could move up to a detached home. Since there was a shortage of new building materials after the war, army surplus products were used in construction. And because most of the appliances and heat were fueled by natural gas, most of the early homes had inadequate electrical wiring. There were all of five basic house models to choose from, initially.

## Shopping: The Pulse of the Community

Shopping was at the core of this Valhalla when the plaza became the first regional (nonmall) shopping center in the South Suburbs. Over time, tiny storefront groceries (such as Roush's in Matteson) went out of business, replaced by the gleaming Jewel supermarket across from the Plaza. Merchants in Chicago Heights, the once-bustling industrial center to the east, quickly succumbed to the glamour of the Plaza. Local department stores went bust one by one as droves marveled at the new styles at Field's and the abundance of hard goods at Sears.

The arc of my life from birth to age twenty-three traveled east and west along U.S. Route 30, better known as Lincoln Highway. Downtown Chicago Heights—where I got my first job as cub reporter at the *Chicago Heights Star* in 1978 after I graduated from the University of Illinois at Chicago—turned into a ghost town, largely smote by the new stores in the plaza. Once graced by banks, jewelry stores, and an elegant Louis Sullivan–designed hotel, "the Heights" fell into permanent decline. Today, even the landmark *Star* building is municipally owned. The only working buildings are the police department (where I spent five days a week doing the police blotter), city hall, the library, and St. James Hospital, where I was born in 1957.

For a time, the success of the plaza sucked the commercial life out of the traditional downtown of Chicago Heights. But when various discount stores began opening up on U.S. Route 30 and Western Avenue, a still-busy intersection, Park Forest acutely felt the pinch. The coup de grace for the plaza was the opening of Lincoln Mall in Matteson in 1973, when I was in high school. Four large department stores anchored the then-massive shopping arena, which was the size of an industrial park. All indoors, it dwarfed the dowager plaza. Matteson then became the economic powerhouse. High-tone Olympia Fields to the north began to absorb wealthier Park Forest residents who outgrew their one-story ranches. Matteson and suburbs to the north and west began to attract even more Park Foresters.

Park Forest serves a watershed role in the history of American suburban communities because it was exceptionally well planned and thrived because of its civic life. It was Olmsted for the baby boom years, sporting everything from walkability to excellent education (I spent one year at Rich East, Park Forest's then-fine high school). The best and the brightest lived there, despite what William Whyte wrote about corporatism in *The Organization Man*. Residents were engaged in their community, and it worked well for so many years. The men (and women) in gray flannel suits were active members of the Kiwanis, Lions, and Rotary clubs and dozens of other civic organizations. Park Forest may have had a commercial, free-enterprise heart, but it gave back generously as a functional civic organism.

Many blamed Lincoln Mall for poaching the heart of Park Forest, but its long-term decay started before the goliath shopping center opened. It fell prey to the American obsession with newness and giantism. Those who wanted bigger and better had nowhere to go in Park Forest. It had no space for mansions or big-box stores. There weren't even enough garages (or lot space to put them on) to house the two-car family's cars and paraphernalia. Yet, what it achieved in its heyday it did brilliantly. Its starter homes were simple and affordable—and still are. It still provides commuter-rail access to the city. You can still ride or bike around it. While it's in the throes of a painful transition in the early twenty-first century, it's a community that still offers some solid arguments for reviving older and perfectly livable inner suburbs.

## The Decline of the Model Suburb

Joan Larsen lived through the rise and fall of Park Forest, which is still struggling to reinvent itself. Much of the town is like Gloria Swanson in *Sunset Boulevard*, a star from another era trying to stay on her feet. The plaza is gone except for a handful of storefronts and a mostly vacant parking lot, which is partially filling up with townhouses in what is now called "Legacy Square," which Larsen dislikes.

When a developer stopped paying property taxes in 1995, the village bought back the plaza properties for $100,000 and back taxes. A decade earlier, the village had created a tax-increment financing district (channeling tax revenues back in to redevelopment) in an attempt to save the plaza. More than $38 million later, the once-glorious hallmark of

DownTown Park Forest, Illinois (formerly a shopping plaza)
*Credit:* Hildy Kingma, village of Park Forest

suburban shopping is now "DownTown Park Forest." The village, twice named an "All-America City" by the National Civic League, demolished 300,000 square feet of retail space, including the long-abandoned Goldblatt's and Sears buildings. Many of the tenants in the downsized core of the old plaza are nonprofits that fill a cultural arts center. "Everyone jumps in a car," Larsen says wistfully when asked about the demise of the plaza. "How do you turn that around? Doesn't it seem that people are brainwashed by the fast pace of life?"

As the 1970s moved American communities into the mall era, Park Foresters drove farther away to do their shopping. Larger discount stores calling themselves Shopper's World and Zayre were built along bustling Route 30 just east of the village. To the west, E.J. Korvette's (then a failing chain where I had worked during college in the late 1970s), the pioneering forerunner of upscale discounters like Target, took even more customers from the plaza in the late 1960s and early 1970s. The plaza was down on its heels by the late 1970s, as even larger malls opened to the north and west of Park Forest. The casual walk to Field's or Sears became a drive down U.S. Route 30 to a host of ever-larger discounters such as Kmart. The heart of Park Forest was decaying as dozens of retailers poached on the plaza's core customers.

Park Forest suffered as residents became more affluent and sought larger homes with more land. It became less of a launching point for affluence and domestic security. During the 1950s and 1960s, serious crime was unheard of in most of Park Forest. What was once a bastion of college-educated corporate employees and professionals is now something more reflective of the South Suburbs. The town, with around thirty thousand residents, is about half African-American, and median housing values were well below the $120,000 for the United States overall and the $130,000 average national selling price of homes in 2007. Like many places experiencing economic decline, it's plagued with drugs, gangs, and shootings. Squatters occupied some empty apartments in 2008.

One shopping center on the city's east side was vacant, awaiting a new developer. Hobbled by a dwindling tax base, village residents have paid one of the highest tax rates in Cook County, the largest and most populous county in the state and third-most populous in the United States. Taxpayers have approved all but one tax-levy increase for the schools in fifty-three years. Some of the older residents have stayed, so the village has tried to accommodate them. One corner of the plaza is buttressed by a high-rise senior-citizen building. The fire department's new, post-modern building seems strangely out of place on another corner. The village Town Hall has moved into the old plaza itself. Except for a barbershop, caterer, movie theater, and a few small shops, the new downtown seems abandoned.

## The Revival

The survival of traditional suburbs like Park Forest is critical in restoring the overall affordability of the U.S. housing market. Older towns that were once bustling bedroom communities have hundreds of thousands of units of viable housing stock. Although the basic Park Forest models are minuscule by today's standards, the village encourages residents to remodel and expand, even offering sample expansion blueprints.

The bleakness of the plaza's skeleton is fading as an entirely new vision for what the village calls its Main Street area is rising from the old plaza's ashes. In an effort to create more housing options, the village sold a portion of the shopping center's footprint to builder Perry Bigelow's company which built sixty-eight houses in part of the plaza's parking lot. The builder is to receive $1 million in reimbursements from the village over ten years from a tax increment financing district, which directs local taxes into this redevelopment project.

Mature communities will also need the experience and insight of builders like Bigelow, whose company is building the Legacy Square homes in the middle of Park Forest. About fifty miles northwest of Park Forest, Bigelow also has developed an entirely new "home town" community in Aurora, Illinois, that builds upon many of the principles established in Park Forest. The towns share a common link: Lincoln Highway, one of the original highways predating the interstates, which meanders thirty-four hundred miles from New York's Times Square to San Francisco's Lincoln Park. (I have a close connection to this road. Chicago Heights, where I was born, was known as the crossroads of America—right where the Lincoln and Dixie Highways intersect.)

When first listed, Bigelow's single-family Park Forest homes ranged in price from $153,000 to $194,000. When you enter one of the Legacy Square homes, the theme is efficiency. Very little space is wasted. The Frontier, a three-bedroom home, could be bought for $160,000, or about $1,000 a month with a $500 down payment. That's well below the national median home price of around $200,000. The price points, somewhat high for Park Forest, are offset by Bigelow's three-year guarantee on home-heating costs. If the bill exceeds $400 during the heating season, the builder will reimburse the homeowner.

Although the homes appear incongruous to the look of the downtown, village officials hope the development will create more population density and support the struggling downtown establishments. A second phase of the home project will add fifty-nine more units on the site of the Field's building. A separate proposed development near the village's commuter rail station calls for 140 condos and almost 60,000 square feet of office and retail space. Although the homes look awkward sitting in the bedraggled parking lot, they represent a new salve for the decay of one of America's aging debutantes. "The focus is to bring everything downtown," says Hildy Kingma, the village's director of economic development and planning. "We're trying to create a center for the community."

## Hometown USA

Unlike Park Forest, Aurora is Illinois's second-largest city with a population of more than 157,000. It's a behemoth that was growing unabatedly at its edges, although its more than century-old downtown is gasping for survival. Once a bustling manufacturer of rail cars and equipment and host to other heavy industries, the City of Lights was incorporated in 1845 and mostly thrived independently of Chicago. Now it spans four counties, has six school districts, and has room for another sixty thousand people, rivaling its prosperous large neighbor to the east, Naperville.

The 1980s weren't kind to Aurora, either, despite the explosion in homebuilding. The loss of manufacturing jobs led to a 16 percent unemployment rate and an increase in the crime rate. In response to the downturn, the city brought in a riverboat casino and built office parks and subdivisions to create some twenty thousand jobs. Still, like old-line Fox Valley cities such as Elgin, the former home of a giant watch-making company, Aurora needed to pump tens of millions of dollars into its decaying downtown. The city fathers, fortunately, were no strangers to progressive change. Before the Civil War, the town started the first free school district in Illinois and was home to hundreds of Sears mail-order houses. The catalog giant sold hundreds of thousands of the kit homes from 1908 to 1940 before the age of the tract development. Aurora was the first city to use electricity for public lighting, hence its nickname.

Bigelow wanted to build an affordable community on Aurora's southern edge where kids could walk to school and parents could walk to work. Although there are few employers in his Town Center, all of his Aurora homes came with his energy guarantee. He claims each of the homes saves 3,550 therms (a measure of heating energy) per year, eliminating twenty tons of carbon dioxide. His design team has incorporated green building techniques gathered from fifteen years of research, landscaping, and land development practices into "HomeTown." More important, Bigelow designed the community to get people outside, one of the core values of New Urbanism, a growing and powerful new movement in development and urban planning (more about this in Chapter 10). Environmental sustainability is built into every one of his homes, although most of the green features are invisible.

To create a tight, energy-stingy building envelope, he's incorporated R-16 wall insulation (R-38 in the attic), which keeps the heat in during the cold months. Sills are sealed at the foundation to prevent air leakage; all of his foundations are insulated to keep the earth's chill from infiltrating the home. The lighting fixtures come standard with energy-efficient compact fluorescent bulbs. His homes mimic some classic American home styles and look very livable, but they're modest and unassuming. They impart a sly charm with model names like "The Barber Shop," which had a starting price of $169,000. For the double-porched, Greek Revival schoolhouse model, the price started at $229,000 at the time of writing.

*Cultural* sustainability is the linchpin in Bigelow's master plan. His approach to integrating social values with environmental concerns is not typical for a builder, and his mission is infused with a dedication to spiritual stewardship. "I believe there's a real God who created the universe and the basic reason for us being on earth is to take care of what God created," Bigelow says of his view toward building in a sustainable manner. "Stewardship is part of my calling in life. As a society, we have a responsibility to design communities so that any hardworking person who's thrifty should have an opportunity to own a home where he or she works."

Bigelow criticizes the trend during the boom for developers and communities to concentrate too heavily on upscale neighborhoods with housing prices that families have since struggled to afford. In many cases, as witnessed by the projected millions of foreclosures that afflicted the U.S. home market, families stretched beyond their financial limits to get into homes, only to lose them. Park Forest and HomeTown were designed to thwart the temptation to overleverage home purchases. "Start out small with something affordable" was the theme for both.

Part of Bigelow's commitment to cultural sustainability is to create communities where there is a diversity of home sizes and price ranges. Smaller houses for singles and double-income couples with no kids (DINKs) comprise 40 percent of HomeTown. When the buyers are ready to move up, they have a choice of larger homes within the community. Bigelow's mortgage counselors help families improve their credit records if they don't immediately qualify. He refused to allow subprime loans for purchasers, and there are no government subsidies for his home buyers. All of the mortgages used to buy Bigelow homes are fixed rate. Although there were foreclosures in HomeTown, the rate is lower than average, he claims.

Bigelow's affordability focus runs counter to the upward mobility of families willing to pay more for homes to gain access to better schools. Aurora schools are far from being top tier, and the city's tax base has taken huge hits from loss of manufacturers over the past thirty years. Like activist Ralph Martire in Chapter 3, Bigelow would like to see school funding unlinked from property taxes.

"Probably the best thing we could do (in the United States) is to reconstruct the property tax system so that it doesn't pay for schools," Bigelow says. "Some communities are not willing to educate other people's kids. They want all the advantages of democracy, yet they don't want *them* to go to *my* schools. Our current approach doesn't make us responsible for our freedoms."

Bigelow practices what he preaches in other ways. He built affordable housing on the blighted west side of Chicago, where he has lived and attended a largely African-American church for several years. Will Bigelow's vision prevail in an industry that has thrived on building boldly upscale subdivisions that have become unsustainable? Perhaps if more builders shared his sense of stewardship—at least in a cultural sense—the spread of spurbs in America would be curtailed.

## The Abandonment of Suburbia

Plenty of real estate has gone vacant because of the unabated move to develop cheap land at the fringe of a metropolis. And the empty storefronts I saw in Aurora and Park Forest were harbingers of what's to come as the contraction of the housing market eats away at overdeveloped areas. Overbuilding of residential and retail buildings makes the cul-de-sac syndrome most pronounced in areas that are economically unsustainable. But it makes solid sense from an urban planning perspective to build or redevelop in places that already have infrastructure in place. Although the elected officials of Park Forest and Aurora consider every opportunity to restore their local economies—further hampered by the housing bust and recession of 2008—they could be rescued by enlightened public policy that shifts resources to older cities and suburbs.

More than four thousand shopping malls in 2008 stood abandoned in the United States. Nearly every growing suburb has been saturated with retail building, and there are more shopping centers than high schools. There was about 20 square feet of shopping space before the bust for every person in America, compared to 2 square feet in Great Britain. Although that's a sure sign of prosperity, the increased spurbing of communities through the building of supercenter stores that occupy several blocks—and kill traditional business districts—contributes to the poaching effect that is harming far too many communities. Since there's a tremendous amount of redundancy, the creative destruction of capitalism means there will be huge losers, and much of the contraction in suburban economies will be concentrated in spurbs that sprung up during the past ten years.

What will happen to the megastores like Home Depot, Lowe's, Wal-Mart, Costco, and others if Americans reach the conclusion some day that it may be simply too expensive to live in the spurbs around which they were built? What will happen to the empty stores? Is it likely they will stay empty or will other big-box retailers move in? My bet is that they will become white elephants and stay vacant for years.

The impact of higher household expenses—including medical, educational, mortgage, food, and energy costs—will have a more profound effect on American spending if the economy continues to contract in the postbust, postcredit crunch era. Since the largest bill for most Americans is housing, Americans will increasingly be attracted to the cities and inner suburbs that have largely been abandoned over the past few decades. From the Pearl District in Portland, Oregon to Washington, DC, a quiet revolution is taking place that rejects the cul-de-sac lifestyle. Townhouse living is replacing the split-level on the quarter-acre lot. Cultural venues in the central city are replacing mowing the lawn and going to the mall.

As noted earlier, it's a challenging task to build affordable homes in places where there's virtually no infrastructure, transportation, services, or amenities nearby. Yet there are thousands of places where builders can still find all of these features. Urban planners call them "infill opportunities." I call them "inner-city neighborhood makeovers," and I'm not referring to the rampant gentrification that seems to plague far too many urban communities.

I didn't have to go far from Park Forest to find one such example. Only a few miles north is the community of South Chicago on the city's southeast side, where the social problems seemed overwhelming, but the neighborhood was fighting to renew itself.

# CHAPTER 9

# Reclaiming the Inner City

SOUTH CHICAGO IS a bereaved ghost of a place, tortured by the echoes of rolling steel mills, machines groaning, men dying, and the mass psychic pain of tens of thousands of lost jobs. I had not seen South Chicago since I left it in 1981, when I had worked my second post-college job as a business and labor reporter for the *Daily Calumet*, a paper that, like the neighborhood, had been deteriorating and closed soon after I left. There I was ushered headlong into the saga of urban decline and the cruel destructiveness of global capitalism.

One of my last assignments for the paper was happenstance. Our paper's photographer, Suza Matczak, listening to the police scanner, heard that a man was holding a woman hostage with a knife on a nearby commuter train. Since I was the police reporter that day, we hopped in her car and saw the Chicago police circling the train at the Hegewisch Station of the South Shore Line railroad, which is surrounded by an industrial wasteland. As James Washington held a knife to the throat of a young woman who just happened to be commuting that day, he demanded to talk with the mayor. Before we had a chance to get any more details from the police, we heard two pops. Washington was hauled out on a stretcher, a sheet covering all but his pristine, white tennis shoes. He had refused to leave the train car and surrender his weapon, so the police felt they had no other choice but to shoot him to save the woman's life.

Washington was unemployed, although the police knew little about him and didn't seem to be in a position to negotiate with him. He may have been one of the tens of thousands laid off from the mills or their supporting industries. I was so shocked at what happened that I didn't think to challenge the police story at the time. I had never seen a man shot to death before—nor have I since. That was one of my last days with the newspaper, so I never found out more about Washington. The drift of my career pulled me away from stories like his, although I'll never cease wondering about the source of his misery. Clearly, he was in a cauldron of despair fueled by economic violence that was battering the once-proud and prosperous community. That day in South Chicago and the last moments of his desperation have never left me.

At the end of America's last great heavy manufacturing age, a devastating recession, undercapitalization, and a global currency rout created the "giant sucking sound," to quote Ross Perot, that took nearly all of the steel jobs out of South Chicago. As billions in capital began to flow into Silicon Valley, Austin, Texas, suburban Boston, Asia, and Mexico, it gushed out of South Chicago like blood from an arterial wound, taking with it the opportunity to elevate thousands of men and women from minimum-wage hell. I witnessed the end of a hundred-year buildup of American industrial prowess. It was as if a once-muscular Vulcan was confined to his deathbed, both literally and symbolically.

One of those death rattles was the abrupt closing of Wisconsin Steel, which had originally opened in 1875 on the banks of the Calumet River, a turgid outlet to Lake Michigan. As the first mill in Chicago, it eventually made steel for the International Harvester Co., the titan that reaped the abundance of the Great Plains to the west. The mill was sold to a shell company called Envirodyne with the aid of a government grant in 1977. By 1980, losing $20 million a year without any investment in the plant's decrepit mills and its largest customer (Harvester, now Navistar International) hobbled by the recession and a strike, Wisconsin Steel locked its gates for good, depriving more than four thousand workers of their last paycheck, pensions, and back pay.

I got to know Wisconsin Steel and its displaced workers better than I knew my own family, since I wrote more than two hundred stories about their futile struggle to get their plant reopened and their benefits paid. I learned about men like Frank Lumpkin, a former bare-knuckle boxer from Wilkes County, Georgia, who came up from the South in hopes of a better-paying job than picking oranges as a sharecropper. He started at the mill in 1949 after serving his country in the U.S. Coast Guard despite not having a birth certificate. Lumpkin, a "scarfer" who removed defects in steel bars, led ex-Wisconsin employees in a sustained effort to regain their jobs and pensions that became known as the Save Our Jobs Committee. They never did regain their former mill positions, but they managed to win back $14.3 million in court settlements after they and Chicago attorney (and my friend) Thomas Geoghegan sued Navistar. The case took seventeen years and recouped only a fraction of what was owed to the workers, estimated at $62 million before Envirodyne filed for bankruptcy.

Lumpkin and his intrepid band of steelworkers did everything they could to get the mill reopened. After a series of would-be buyers paraded through and disappeared, most of the mill was demolished. Every politician promised the workers the moon. On one steelworker bus trip to Washington to lobby Congress, I was told by then-Congressman Gus Savage (the self-proclaimed Muhammad Ali of congressmen), as I rode in his car down Pennsylvania Avenue, that he would help the steelworkers. Savage had a problem just showing up for votes and did almost nothing for the jobless.

## Jobs, a Community's Anchor

When a large employer shuts its doors, it's devastating to a community. South Chicago at the time was no different from Detroit, Cleveland, Dayton, Pittsburgh, or any industrial enclave whose manufacturing jobs were permanently leaving the country. Once part of a steelmaking region that girdled Lake Michigan from Waukegan to near the Michigan border, South Chicago was brought to its knees by shutdowns of the legendary Pullman railcar plant, Republic Steel, and U.S. Steel's South Works, which at its height employed more than twenty thousand workers.

Pullman was once so large that its owner George Pullman created an entire community for the workers. The rail baron's utopia quickly became a workers' prison when it became clear he controlled everything in town, including rents, which were inflated. A violent strike was broken by federal troops in 1894, launching the careers of labor leader Eugene Debs and a young lawyer named Clarence Darrow.

By the time the personal computer age dawned, more than thirty thousand jobs had left the area, sending thousands of people onto the welfare rolls. Workers like Raymond Gutierrez went from a decent mill job with health insurance, a pension, and an hourly wage above $20 an hour to parking cars and bagging groceries for $3.25 an hour. Countless thousands went back to Mexico, had to depend on their wives' or family members' incomes, or committed suicide. After the industrial corridor of South Chicago collapsed in the 1980s, desperation became the employer of choice as good-paying union jobs gave way in the Reagan era to a raft of employers who were more than willing to hire at non-living wages.

The only large industrial employer remaining is the Ford Motor Co.'s Torrence Avenue plant, which opened in the late 1920s but was imperiled as of early 2009. A handful of viable mills that survived the 1980s eventually were bought by foreign companies such as ArcelorMittal after massive benefit and wage cuts. Although the industrial Jerusalem that was South Chicago now consists of acres of ruins, the neighborhoods that made up the southeast corner of the city are fighting valiantly for survival.

## The Rebuilding

With an ample smile and plenty of persistence, Angela Hurlock was one of the stolid souls who had come to rebuild South Chicago one house at a time. As the executive director of Claretian Associates, she was running a housing program that seeks to build quality affordable and green housing in one of the most challenging urban settings. The Claretian Catholic order has run the nearby Our Lady of Guadalupe Church and the National Shrine of St. Jude since 1924. (St. Jude is the patron saint of hopeless causes.) The church was one of the few neighborhood institutions left standing after the carnage of the 1980s.

The Claretians began work in the early 1990s to provide housing for those who couldn't afford to move out of the impoverished neighborhood, starting with the fifty-three-unit Villa Guadalupe Senior Services apartment building for those over fifty-five. It was the first residential construction in South Chicago in more than a decade. Rents for low-income tenants were subsidized by a private $1.5 million endowment fund and vouchers from the Chicago Low-Income Trust Fund.

Hurlock was working in her native West Side neighborhood when she accepted the Claretian position. With a master's in architecture and an MBA, and halfway through a master's in urban planning, she had worked in a small architecture firm and studied in Paris before coming to South Chicago. She speaks Spanish and French fluently. "The West Side was similar to South Chicago," Hurlock says. "It had a small-town feel." Hurlock and her husband were so committed to South Chicago that they moved into a section of the neighborhood called Millgate, which was only a few blocks from the now completely razed site of U.S. Steel's South Works main entry, which occupied prime lakefront property from 79th Street to 95th Street from 1901 to 1992. The South Chicago that Hurlock hoped to save was not faring well. With no new employers coming in, dilapidated housing stock, and rising crime, she was fighting a headwind. Only 55 percent of people over sixteen were in the workforce then, compared to about 70 percent for the United States overall. More than 17 percent of families were living below the poverty line, compared to 9 percent nationally. The average home was worth $90,000 or less.

Based on the idea "that everyone wants to live in a safe neighborhood," Hurlock began to improve housing and create streets that people would want to live on again. The nucleus of what made South Chicago a great neighborhood for services was still there, so she didn't have to start from scratch. A jewelry store where her husband bought her wedding ring was two blocks away. A drug store, banks, post office, and two schools were within walking distance from their home. To get downtown, there was a commuter train stop.

The 2,200-square-foot two-flat (a residential building suitable for two families) that Hurlock bought in 2005 was an energy-efficient house built in the third phase of the Claretian homes project. She pays about $500 a year for heating costs in an area that averages up to $150 per *month*. Her neighbors pay more than $300 per month during heating season. Hurlock sees green homes as not only good for the environment but also a model of affordability, especially for low-income residents who are hit hardest by rising utility bills. Multifamily housing—such as her own two-flat—also reduces living expenses by offering shared housing costs.

When you walk through the neighborhood, the Claretian homes don't stand out. They are basic frame homes that have elevated entrances because of the vaulted sidewalks that were originally built over the mud flats on which the neighborhood was situated. More than half of the labor force for the Claretian homes was recruited from the neighborhood and trained locally in the YouthBuild USA program. In 2007, the Claretians

finished two-flats and single-family homes. The larger units sold for
$235,000 and the smaller ones for $165,000. By comparison, similar
homes on the North Side of the city could sell for two to three times that
much. Hurlock hopes to help redevelop more than eighty lots.

It's clear from the neighborhood's battered blocks that Hurlock is
making no more than a dent in solving South Chicago's housing woes.
Dozens of boarded-up buildings and homes should be demolished,
which is the city's preference, creating more empty lots among the more
than ten thousand sitting idle. Inner cities face a chronic shortage of
affordable housing as it is: An estimated five million rental units are
needed for those who can't afford even a basic home. According to the
National Low Income Housing Coalition, some 16 million live in substandard housing, pay more than half of their income for shelter, or are
homeless. "It's difficult to house families and keep homeowners in their
homes," Hurlock says with a sigh. "Those scared out of homes due to
foreclosures [enter] the rental market and that increases the need for
rental housing."

The City of Chicago has committed funds and several agencies to
help South Chicago rebound. Working with local groups, it created a
special taxing district to spend $4 million to fix the crumbling vaulted
sidewalks. Millions of dollars have been poured into rehabbing buildings along the neighborhood's Commercial Avenue business district.
And teams of local activists and city officials have organized jobs and
child care centers, and small-business redevelopment. A contractors'
association has called for the construction of three hundred new homes
and rehabilitation of 250 buildings. A housing collaboration with the
Claretians is providing a pool for home mortgages. Through an integrated approach, the Southeast Chicago Development Commission and
its partners are hoping to rebuild the neighborhood through a "quality
of life" plan that focuses on local job creation, services, and housing.
There's also a program to wean families from welfare payments.

## Barriers to Revival

The obstacles in the way of battling decay are substantial in South
Chicago just as they are from South Central Los Angeles to Newark.
Street violence is a consistent and unforgiving predator. South Chicago
consistently ranks among the most violent of the city's neighborhoods.

At least twelve street gangs are active on the Southeast Side, which has spawned a wave of murders throughout the city; an alarmingly high percentage of them are of schoolchildren.

More than thirty-two students were killed in 2007 (twenty more shot by midyear 2008, at about two per week), prompting Chicago schools to spend more than $55 million on security for its more than four hundred thirty-five thousand pupils in six hundred schools. With the vicious cycle of unemployment come violence and the sense that it can't be escaped. It reproduces like a virus, with devastating consequences. Gang- and drug-related shootings are ravaging inner cities. In Chicago, five people a day (on average) were shot in 2007, most of them in a handful of police districts. Murder has been the leading cause of death for African-Americans between the ages of fifteen and thirty-four for the past quarter century. "Each shooting, each murder, leaves a devastating legacy," writes long-time urban observer Alex Kotlowitz, "and a growing school of thought suggests that there's little we can do about the entrenched urban poverty if the relentless pattern of street violence isn't broken."

In troubled neighborhoods, social turmoil has a direct economic impact. Working families move out, leaving concentrated poverty. That lowers home values, which in turn cuts the amount of money available for schools. That dynamic contributes to the disparity between urban and suburban schools. In 2008, some 65 percent of neighborhoods were not only segregated by race, they were separated by educational opportunities as well. Even if poorer city residents wanted to access jobs in the suburbs, they are physically separated due to lack of transportation from 40 percent of the jobs lying more than ten miles from the city center, according to the Brookings Institution.

The meanest streets won't be any more secure unless jobs and neighborhood safety return to places like South Chicago. It's unlikely, though, that any new manufacturing employers will be relocating there. Long term, the United States is still experiencing an avalanche of losses in its manufacturing employment sector: More than fifty-four thousand goods-producing jobs were lost in April 2008 alone, marking the twentieth consecutive negative month for manufacturing occupations. That left about half the population of South Chicago unemployed during any thirty-day period. If older blue-collar areas were given more attention by the mainstream media, they could easily have qualified for their own Great

Depression by 2008. The bust of 2008 saw the greatest amount of unemployment overall in thirty years.

Perhaps only large-scale, integrated inner-city developments that attract jobs along with wealthier new residents will revive working-class neighborhoods. South Chicago may witness a massive makeover in the form of the South Works site, a 586-acre parcel that's larger than the entire Chicago Loop central business district, and it's right on Lake Michigan. The city originally selected the giant architectural and planning firm Skidmore, Owings & Merrill to create a master plan for the site, which still had not been released as this book went to press. This was the firm that designed Sears Tower, which was built using steel *made* in South Works, making structural products for many of the world's skyscrapers for 112 years before it closed in 1992. I hope that irony will not be lost on the developers of the site.

To facilitate the development, the city had relocated the fabled U.S. 41, which snakes its way through Chicago along Lake Shore Drive and travels from the Canadian border to Miami. When I visited

A zero-energy South Chicago home
*Credit:* Angela Hurlock, Claretian Associates

in 2008, that section of the drive that goes through the site had been fenced off as if it was a toxic waste dump. If the project is completed, it is expected to include a marina, restaurants, retail shopping, and community centers. It's not known (at this writing) whether the new homes there will be green or affordable or when the project might be completed.

Undaunted, Hurlock continues her work just west of the planned mega development. The first three phases of the Claretian project consisted of thirty homes that were priced as low as $145,000. Like Victor Zaderej's home (see Chapter 6), the Claretian homes have structural insulated panels for walls, boosting overall energy performance and lowering labor costs. Any openings are sealed and caulked to prevent air leakage.

The R-value of the roof insulation is a generous 42.5, and it's almost 30 for the walls (R-value is a measure of the quality of insulation; the higher the R-value, the better the insulation). Twelve of the initial homes have electricity-generating solar panels, which produce 1.2 kilowatts of power. Although that's not enough juice for the entire home (the panels provide only up to 22 percent of total power needs), it can offset electrical bills. The cost of the $14,000 solar systems was reduced by federal and state subsidies. Energy-efficient windows, appliances, and recycled carpeting and wallboard complete the package. Since so few of them were built, the homes cost about 5 percent more than conventional houses of that size, including various subsidies. If mass-produced, they would cost less than stick-built homes. The greatest benefit comes in the form of utility bills that are half the average homeowner's.

Claretian has expanded its housing mission to South Chicago apartment buildings as well. Its Casa Kirk development houses twenty-nine families, including some that were formerly homeless. Hurlock is also working on rehabilitating other buildings and counseling prospective homeowners. Her organization has even helped build a "people's park" that came together with more than three thousand hours of volunteer labor. The charming little enclave represents the hard work that continues to be needed to revive South Chicago. Some two hundred cubic yards of garbage had to be removed from the three "abandoned and desecrated" vacant lots where the park stands. Now there's a community gathering place with flowers, shrubs, benches, and a mosaic mural created by local children. As inspiring as Hurlock's work is, it will take more than targeted charity and community redevelopment to recycle and rebuild American cities' ample supplies of housing stock and bring them back on the market at affordable prices.

## The Affordability Crunch

The long-term erosion of living-wage employment drove millions from cities. Once-thriving neighborhoods couldn't stand on their own anymore because they couldn't offer steady jobs. Employers either moved out of the country or chose to locate within white-collar bastions in far-out suburbs. Suburbs absorbed a great many of the upwardly mobile residents and left cities bereft.

As those who could afford to move farther from inner suburbs and city cores did so, the economic diversity and strength of the neighborhoods they left behind deteriorated. City neighborhoods became weaker during this decline. Only 23 percent of central-city neighborhoods in the twelve largest areas had a middle-income profile in 2000. Even before the housing boom of the twenty-first century began, the larger trend was the ghettoization of income classes. Unlike Park Forest, where anyone could have lived next door to an executive or PhD researcher in the 1950s through the 1970s, in this century, it's more likely that homeowners will be living next door to someone who makes as much as they do. When home-equity values soared during the boom, those who did the best either upgraded to larger homes farther out or bought second and third homes in other boom markets.

Flush with home-equity cash, move-up buyers often spent lavishly and went into more debt for the upgraded digs. They tended to be older than first-time buyers—forty-five versus thirty-three—and almost always had higher incomes. The average move-up buyer made $84,170 a year versus $64,000 for first-timers. In keeping with the American progressive economic spirit, they wanted more house and were willing to pay for it—even though they may not have needed the additional room and expense. The median square footage for the upgrader was 2,000 square feet, compared with 1,500 for the first-timers. Move-up buyers paid almost $100,000 more for that bigger and better home and certainly got hit later with higher property taxes and the overall expenses of maintaining, heating, cooling, and powering a larger domicile.

Did the move-up purchasers really get more for their money or did they just go deeper into debt thinking that appreciation would bail them out in the future in a better neighborhood? In many cases they did worse financially while the neighborhoods they left didn't fare well either.

As the largest portion of household budgets, housing has mushroomed into an ever-larger expense, which became even more burdensome during this century's first half-decade. More than one-third of homeowners with a mortgage are paying 30 percent or more of their gross income in housing costs. For a family grossing $100,000, that means $30,000 or more is going to pay the mortgage. What's left over is needed to cover taxes, insurance, food, and other necessities. It's not surprising that hundreds of thousands of homeowners tapped their home equity to spend on discretionary items. They had no money left over after paying for fixed costs, so they dipped into the well to cover their spending—or to pay old bills.

The housing boom only exacerbated the housing affordability crisis, especially in inner cities and suburbs. Thousands were priced out of the large cities where gentrification occurred, with the most acute problems seen on the West and East Coasts. That pushed families ever farther from their jobs in a quest to find a home that they could barely afford. In the inner city, the pain was twice felt since housing authorities were in the throes of demolishing public housing.

Core urban neighborhoods were not generating quality, affordable housing to replace the vertical ghettos being torn down. Lagging inflation by a huge percentage, the minimum wage provided no relief for those trying to keep up with housing costs. The National Low Income Housing Coalition found that "nowhere does a minimum-wage job provide enough income for a household to afford the fair market rental for a two-bedroom house."

From Los Angeles to New York, affordable housing may be the most pressing social finance issue of the twenty-first century. More than 14 million people had critical housing needs as of late 2008. Those earning close to the minimum wage in the Northeast, California, or any number of coastal areas where home prices soared during the boom were hurt the most. An *entry-level* home in California in the fourth quarter of 2007 was priced at more than $411,000, which basically bought a two-bedroom ranch in a modest neighborhood. What would be an upscale home throughout most of the South is downright tiny in southern California. A home buyer would need at least $82,200 in income with

10 percent down at 6.2 percent (adjustable-rate mortgage [ARM]) to qualify for that home. The monthly payment would be almost $3,000, including taxes and insurance. The $36,000 in yearly house expenses would absorb nearly half of the owner's income. And that's for a starter home with exposure to the bond market through the ARM. If rates went up and the buyers couldn't cover the higher payment, they'd be sunk. That was what happened when rates rose on ARMs in late 2007. In California alone, only one-third of all households could afford a starter home.

Add closing costs to the list price of a home, and the transaction becomes even more difficult for most lower- or middle-income buyers. Total origination and closing costs average $3,400. That's in addition to the average $2,550 down payment, according to the U.S. Department of Housing and Urban Development (HUD). Embedded in those costs are the real estate brokerage fee of 6 percent or less and $1,200 in title insurance fees. And if you're only high school educated, Latino, or African-American, you'll pay even more, HUD found: up to $2,300 more. Until Congress takes a hard look at all of the fixed costs of housing—and acts to reduce these often-onerous expenses and the rampant discrimination—the American dream will remain out of reach for millions.

## The Steep Cost of the Exodus

The high price of housing was one of the great drivers behind suburban development and will always be a factor in American homeownership. Ever since the dawn of the twentieth century, families all over the country were desperate to leave crowded city apartments for a place of their own. That's part of the American dream that has been largely enjoyed by almost 70 percent of the country. Yet there's been a cost to this relentless push to places that had been farm fields only years earlier. Millions of Americans got caught in a financial cul-de-sac as they tried to pay for their house far outside the city.

To create infrastructure where previously there was only soil costs everyone. Places like Chicago, where there had been (paid for) streets, sewers, and sidewalks for more than one hundred years, began to depopulate. Cook County lost seventy-three thousand people between 2000 and 2005, according to the Census Bureau. That made the home county of Chicago the biggest loser among all U.S. counties (during that time).

Where did the people go? They went to collar counties like Kendall, southwest of Joliet (more than twenty miles from Chicago), which was the fastest-growing county in the U.S. toward the end of 2007. Neighboring Will and Grundy counties also experienced heady growth. Those who moved out of state headed to sunny Phoenix or Florida, where land and homes were cheap and taxes low. Those who remained "up north" were chasing lower housing prices and jobs far from the cities. Who can blame them? But they may fall behind economically in the long run as the higher costs of living in the hinterlands will catch up with them.

Lower- and middle-income families often fare the worst in most outer suburbs. As 2007's *State of the Nation's Housing* from Harvard notes, "Even for households that make long commutes to reduce their housing costs, the spending constraints are significant. Indeed, bottom-quartile families with low housing outlays spent almost four times more on transportation than those with high housing outlays."

The study adds that service workers who used to live in affordable city neighborhoods were facing "severe housing cost burdens" in the suburbs. They had to spend a higher proportion of their income on the cost of owning and maintaining a home. So the child-care workers, nursing aides, elementary teachers, police officers, and firefighters who might have been living comfortably in the city were struggling outside of it. The study estimates that more than 37 million people faced housing affordability problems, a record level that was made worse by the housing boom. This number will likely fall as home prices recede, but it points to a much larger debt affliction linked to housing affordability.

Mortgages in 2008 made up about 73 percent of all household debt, compared to 65 percent in 2000. That's why families would do anything to cut that expense. During the boom, the credit markets, mortgage mavens, and Wall Street financial engineers heard their pleas and sold interest-only and option adjustable rate mortgages. Although these loans didn't build any principal through monthly payments, they were extremely popular in the most expensive areas. They accounted for more than 30 percent of all originations in California, Nevada, Colorado, and Arizona, places where price appreciation well exceeded the national average.

Undoubtedly there were hundreds of thousands of cases of under-writing abuses and fraud. Brokers who had only financial incentives for *closing* loans frequently had no interest in ensuring that a client could afford the loan long term (particularly if the rate adjusted higher). The once-dominant fixed-rate loan, which accounted for 84 percent of all loans in 2001, yielded to adjustables, which made up 55 percent of all loans in 2006 and became a trillion-dollar industry of their own.

## Rampant Exploitation

Who got hurt the most in the financing "revolution"? Those who could least afford the catastrophic rate resets in 2007 and beyond. Originally billed as the most affordable options, adjustables ensnared hundreds of thousands with higher costs and inflexible terms. Although the subprime crisis ravaged areas from San Bernardino County, California, to Miami, more of these high-cost mortgages were issued in the Chicago area than any other place, according to the *Chicago Reporter*, a well-respected investigative newsletter that focuses on community issues.

Ironically, most of these mortgages were issued in areas where mortgages were typically denied. During the subprime boom, home prices in these communities skyrocketed artificially. By 2008, every area dominated by subprime lending was facing record foreclosures. Such areas will be the last to recover. Not only do abandoned homes lead to higher crime rates and lower tax revenues, they are like a cancer that spreads to neighboring homes. One study from the Woodstock Institute found that from 1997 through 1998, almost four thousand foreclosures in Chicago reduced property values in neighboring homes by nearly $600 million, or an average of $159,000 per home. In California, foreclosure-related price erosion dropped prices by one-third to one-half.

Combined with high unemployment and declining housing values, foreclosures will continue to blight communities in profound ways. Predatory lending, which targeted those with poor credit history, only exacerbated the ravaging of these neighborhoods. Borrowers who obtained overpriced loans paid up to 3 percentage points more than people with better credit who were granted conventional, prime-rate loans. The gouging targeted blacks and Hispanics, who received almost 50 percent of these loans. Even African-American households making more than $100,000 were more likely to get caught in this scam than white homeowners making less than $35,000 a year.

About half of those who received the high-cost loans could have qualified for prime mortgages. The obese bonuses and salaries of mortgage bankers came at the expense of homeowners who could least afford the loans they received. And the ill effects of the mortgage giveaway weren't confined to lower-middle-class areas. Banks were happy to lend to investors. Some 60 percent of the mortgages foreclosed on in Las Vegas in 2007 were held by nonresidents. Vacation-home sales, which rose 18 percent from 2002 to 2007, also got caught in the mortgage meltdown. The mortgage industry, enabled by Wall Street's money-packaging machine, spread the loan money around like buttons at a campaign rally.

## Moving Forward

Neighborhoods like South Chicago (or any inner-city area that's targeted for redevelopment) can experience a revival because they offer affordability and accessibility to city services. They will have to overcome a number of daunting hurdles, though, which may take decades. Yet I don't believe it will require a massive bailout from the federal government akin to President Johnson's "urban renewal" programs of the 1960s. Cities offer a tremendous value relative to new ex-urban developments because transportation, services, and infrastructure are already there. Private developers have slowly embarked upon inner-city redevelopment with a number of success stories. Nearly every major city can boast of an inner-city neighborhood that was "regentrified" in some way.

This largely unheralded national urban revival, which took a back seat to suburban growth during the housing boom, may be slowed by economic downturns but will expand with time. Americans of all ages will want to walk and bike more, abandon their cars, and shop locally. A Coldwell Banker real estate broker survey in 2008 found that 80 percent of those polled wanted to live in cities because of higher fuel costs. Although energy prices will always influence short-term thinking, the demographic reality of more Americans desiring less commuting and more walkability will be the largest force behind this trend.

Inner-city neighborhoods will be the biggest beneficiary of the rediscovery of cities and older suburbs. Local planners and government officials, sensing that this trend can help them revitalize blighted areas, have already begun to capitalize on this movement. Here are some prime examples:

➤ San Mateo, California, has converted a downtown section into a livable transit hub. An old department store has been converted into a "village" of six hundred residential units.

➤ Fort Myers, Florida, whose metropolitan area was burned by the housing bust, is rebuilding its downtown along New Urbanism principles. A shopping area and residential units are being redesigned.

➤ Established cities such as Washington, DC, Boston, New York, Philadelphia, Chicago, and Seattle are undergoing transformations by which downtowns and stable neighborhoods are becoming even more "walkable," that is, pedestrian *and* bicycle friendly. Many of these cities already have functioning public transit and interurban commuter rail systems.

➤ Urban redevelopment is also benefiting from businesses moving their corporate campuses from far-out suburbs to inner cities. When the footwear company Adidas moved from a suburban Portland (Oregon) location to an old hospital site in the city, it brought eight hundred employees and a raft of neighborhood improvements.

➤ Light-rail systems have improved the quality of life for rapidly growing cities such as Atlanta; Portland, Oregon; Houston; Denver; and Miami. Where there is efficient, street-level public transportation, there is less need for cars and parking lots. It makes a city much more livable.

Ultimately, the combination of strong public transportation systems, pedestrian and bike friendly streets, mixed-use zoning, and locally owned businesses could be part of a formula for renewed real estate development in the most neglected areas.

The same value renowned investor Warren Buffett finds in unglamorous, mature companies, like railroads, utilities, and insurance firms, developers will find in inner cities. They've already discovered opportunities in nearly every city that stands a chance of rebounding. But they will need incentives to rebuild from every level of government and the U.S. tax code. There needs to be a shift away from subsidizing spurb-friendly highway projects, and more tax dollars need to be moved into inner suburbs and cities. In a philosophical sense, urban planners and policymakers need to adopt a holistic attitude in making housing and communities more human in scale, safe, and affordable. A handful of developers, planners, and builders have already adopted this enlightened approach.

# CHAPTER 10

# Sustainability and Development
## Bridging the Gap

WATCHING THE GENTLE eddies and current of the Mississippi River revived me as I took a respite from a conference on green building sponsored by the National Association of Home Builders in St. Louis. The city is a perfect symbolic spot to hold it. Jefferson sent his emissaries Lewis and Clark to this place more than two hundred years ago. The two explorers entered the mouth of the Missouri with their flatboat just north of the city to conduct one of the largest real estate surveys in history. The conference is a block away from the Jefferson National Expansion Memorial, the Gateway Arch, and the Old Courthouse, where the then-slave Dred Scott sued for—and lost—his freedom (he was later freed). That was the famous Supreme Court case that essentially denied his citizenship and humanity and gave a virtual carte blanche to the spread of slavery. And to the west, millions immersed themselves in the glory and heartbreak of Jefferson's real estate bonanza.

St. Louis was my portal to William McDonough, an enlightened beacon of a man who embodies the ideals of Jefferson, Frederick Law Olmsted, John Muir, Buckminster Fuller, and Frank Lloyd Wright. Although many know him mostly as a green architect, he's the Leonardo da Vinci of green design and is busy designing entire Chinese cities that will house 14 million people. His vision merges environmental design into everything from skyscrapers to the clothes we wear. Working with a chemist, he's formed a company that focuses on "cradle-to-cradle" products that provide "technical nutrients" that can be recycled and reused and won't be toxic to the environment (Michelle Kaufmann is working with him on green materials for her homes). He's won numerous awards for his work, including a presidential citation for sustainable development.

McDonough made the cover of *Time* magazine as someone who is "changing the design of the world." President George W. Bush was so impressed with one of his White House presentations that he asked McDonough to repeat it for several agency heads, although it had little impact on the antienvironment Bush appointees.

McDonough is the kind of thinker who has done the heavy lifting of sustainable design. The architect retained a steady, calming tone as he breezed through his PowerPoint slides at the green building conference, which made Al Gore's Oscar-winning presentation look like a quotidian trade-show pitch. He resembles Steve Forbes, the publisher, although he's considerably more modest in his mien. He dresses like a rumpled country lawyer, preferring bow ties to cravats, and has this serene aura around him. Like many of the green visionaries of his generation, McDonough frames nearly all of his plans in terms of environmental impact and economic logic.

## Measuring Environmental Impact

What does a building or product do to the earth? Does it work for it or against it? One of McDonough's largest-scale industrial projects was redesigning Ford Motor Co.'s River Rouge plant, which was a sprawling, pollution-spewing complex south of Detroit. Incorporating McDonough's design to retain water and respect the local environment, the site employs one of the largest green roofs in the world, which McDonough claims saved Ford at least $35 million in waste-treatment costs. One of his slides shows killdeer eggs in the middle of the roof, to which McDonough quips, "We now have 350-pound autoworkers learning bird songs."

McDonough's credo broadly embraces a combination of aesthetic, political, and human needs. He tells his audience that his work must "delight, for a diverse, safe, healthy, and just world with clean air, water, soil, and power. It should also be economically equitable, ecologically elegant, and enjoyable." He employs a triangle diagram to show how "ecology, equity, and economy" relate to each other. It is an equilateral triangle. No component takes precedence over another. Each side equally supports the polygon of his manifesto.

Born in Tokyo in 1951, McDonough has early memories of oxcarts rolling in and out of the still-devastated city, bringing out "night soil" to be recycled in farm plots. Between years at Dartmouth and Yale, he worked for King Hussein in Jordan and became fascinated with the airflow through Bedouin tents. Despite being colored black and sitting in the middle of a desert, they created a convection that circulated air within. From there, he discovered the caves of Petra and their ancient water system. He later built the first of his three solar homes in Ireland (not known for its solar resources).

Early notoriety in his architectural practice came when he designed the first green office building, for the Environmental Defense Fund, in 1984. After designing a $200 million office tower in Warsaw in 1989, he boldly suggested that the developer plant $100,000 worth of trees to offset the pollution the building would create. A *New Yorker* cartoon would later spoof his suggestion: One executive asks another, "How many trees do I have to plant to atone for my pollution?"

Venturing further into the difficult space between sustainability and development, McDonough helped write the Hannover Principles, a set of guidelines for sustainable development. "Optimal sustainability is looking at the perfectly exquisite to achieve the perfectly impossible," he declared in his presentation after discussing Einstein, making safe plastics, and examining some eight thousand chemicals at the Ciba-Geigy corporation for their impacts on the environment across their life cycles. No component of production can be excused when considering the web of life.

McDonough's daunting list of objectives in detoxifying the environment and making the planet habitable for eternity is dizzying. Yet, like a symphony, he pulls you back into a basic theme. We can design, manufacture, and build with "ecological intelligence." That means paying attention to where something has been, how it's used, and where it ends up. His book *Cradle to Cradle* explores the idea of products that can become part of the biological food chain—plastics that are more than recycled because they're never wasted in the industrial process.

To like-minded thinkers like energy guru Amory Lovins, green capitalist Paul Hawken, and futurist Hazel Henderson, the need to see how nature and manmade operations are systems of systems is essential. A wetland is a processor within a watershed. It stores, filters, and purifies water. It's not an island of activity. It works within a larger environmental system. If we want to abandon cul-de-sac thinking, we have to do holistic planning and design.

## The Re-Imagined Home

In re-imagining the home, McDonough and builders and architects of ecodynamic structures use the same construct. A green home isn't *just* a structure with solar panels adorning the roof. It is a consciously designed, interacting entity. It retains heat through thermal mass. Stones can capture solar energy and release the warmth at night. Where water is often scarce, an ecodynamic home channels water from the roof into a cistern or onto a green roof that can grow plants.

When the home has outlived its useful life, like a tree that has fallen to the forest floor, it can be easily disassembled. Buckminster Fuller, the iconoclastic engineer-designer-thinker, built such a home in the 1930s. Dubbing it the "dymaxion home," it was based on aeronautical construction and could be easily moved and taken apart. But it looked like an aluminum flying saucer, and it never quite took off. McDonough paid homage to the inventor in one brief slide, and then reiterated his credo. The builders gave him a standing ovation.

When I asked McDonough if he thought Fuller was still relevant, he agreed and presented the concept that's anathema to most builders: "precise, manufactured housing." Although he didn't articulate that theme in his talk to the builders, the industry has always chafed at this idea, often deriding modular construction as building glorified mobile homes. As a result of the builders' hostility—and negative public perception—modular housing has never been more than a tiny niche market.

Living in a home in Charlottesville, Virginia, designed by Thomas Jefferson, McDonough built his first five houses by hand. Extending Jefferson's basic tenet of the pursuit of happiness, he includes in every one of his talks the precept that "design is the first signal of human intention." "Nowhere in the Bill of Rights does it say we have a right to pollute," McDonough tells the builders, expanding on his Jefferson riff. "Isn't pollution a design problem? Isn't regulation a design failure?"

### McDonough's Vision in the New Energy Age

Several months after the first McDonough talk I attended, I returned to Oak Park, Illinois, the home of Frank Lloyd Wright's first studio and many of his Prairie-style homes, to hear McDonough speak again at Wright's Unity Temple. Light streamed in at multiple angles through abstract, art-glass windows like rays in a Titian painting as McDonough relished the honor of speaking in Wright's more-than-century-old cubist masterpiece. I wanted to know how McDonough would address the needs of a world where oil prices had soared past $140 a barrel, the price of gasoline was hitting record highs, and the value of U.S. residential real estate was still sinking. He again invoked Jefferson's dictums that "the earth belongs to the living" and that these conditions are "a tragedy of our own making."

Although I'm usually sympathetic to the message, after hearing McDonough talk about dying coral reefs, toxic chemicals, and carbon dioxide buildups in the oceans, and noting that according to him the sun provides "about five thousand times more nuclear energy daily than we'll ever need," I was starved for details on how to end our woes at the nadir of our carbon age—what political and personal actions were required? His stump speech won't cut it. How can all of his ideas come together in redesigning the American home? How do we cure the cul-de-sac syndrome in which building and growth have been offered as the answers to everything?

Ecodynamic design—so that buildings recycle rain and wastewater, are solar powered and heated, and have lower rates of energy consumption—is part of the puzzle, although I've heard that before. Reusing materials such as glass, wallboard, lumber, and plastics can also be part of the plan, as they are in Kaufmann's homes (and any custom green home). Yet these will not necessarily make homes more affordable. If anything, greening a home typically adds to the cost. What about redesigning *communities* on a human scale to reduce vehicle and resource use?

"In many ways, the environmental crisis is a design crisis," Sim Van der Ryn states in his seminal *Ecological Design*. "It is a consequence of how things are made, buildings are constructed, and landscapes are used. . . . Such myopic design cannot fail to degrade the living world, and, by extension, our own health." Van der Ryn employed many of the lowest-tech ideas in the Farallones Institute's "Integral Urban House" in Berkeley, California, in the 1980s.

Much of McDonough's and Van der Ryn's observations are old news, though. Such criticisms were lodged decades ago when tie-dyed shirts were in fashion the *first* time, yet few mainstream policy makers have linked the *design* of the American city and suburb to the environmental end game. The main targets have been petroleum and coal combustion, pollution, and carbon dioxide release. Too much attention has been paid to environmental *outputs* and not enough to *inputs*. Translating that from engineering jargon, we've not designed homes and communities to work sustainably.

When McDonough reminds his audiences that "we are Thomas Jefferson's seventh generation," he also reassures capitalists that "we don't need to choose between environmental responsibility and economic sustainability." They can be compatible, but it will take comprehensive planning and design to rethink, restructure, and rebuild the American home and community, so that they are responsible users of the planet's limited resources. If we get this right, it will help everyone prosper, create affordable housing, and foster a healthy environment from Beijing to Boston.

## The Spurb Shakeout: A New Urbanism Agenda

The successful marriage of economic and ecological sustainability will do much to make American housing growth viable in every metropolitan area. Yet it will take vision, new laws, a reordering of federal subsidies, and an enlightened way of seeing development to make it a livable, healthy reality in every urban area.

The New Urbanism movement, which loosely embraces "smart growth," "sensible development," and comprehensive community planning (names of different branches of urban planning that overlap), is one vehicle that can help get America's housing markets back on a sustainable track. Demographics will play a key role in a revival of forward-looking urban planning, as will higher energy prices.

Empty nesters will join singles in an odd alliance to reject spurbs and revitalize the American dream. They will opt for vibrant night life and compact neighborhoods with walkable amenities and accessible public transportation. This shift will channel an exodus from tract-home heaven back into core cities and mature suburbs with viable downtowns. In examining this demographic trend, Arthur Nelson of the Metropolitan Institute of Virginia Tech estimates that it will create a surplus of 22 million large-lot homes (on a sixth of an acre or more) by 2025—that's 40 percent of the supply of these kinds of homes on the market. What will happen to the spurbs? They may start to resemble the abandoned inner suburbs that were vacated over the past twenty years. Their quality of life, tax base, and population will decline. Areas now plagued by foreclosures may take decades to recover—if they do at all.

Akin to McDonough's philosophy, the thinking behind rebuilding communities will be both radical and traditional. By *traditional* I don't mean the business-as-usual cul-de-sac subdivisions with huge lots and no transportation access other than one road through a faux gate. I'm referring to the old-style neighborhoods where you could safely walk and bike to most retail locations. There would also be a train, bus line, or bike trail system connecting the community to the rest of the world.

These "new-old" developments would also be more energy efficient because their residents would be using public transportation, walking and biking more, and driving less. At about $4 a gallon for gasoline, that means a savings of almost $6 billion on fuel alone. A public transit rider consumes half as much gasoline as someone who drives all the time. In the best of all new urbanist worlds, we would walk, bike, and use public transportation more, but only 5 percent of the U.S. population lives close enough to commuter systems to avail themselves of their benefits. Nevertheless, 90 percent of public transit agencies reported increases in ridership in mid-2008 and one-third of the demand for new homes was focused on walkable communities.

Urban enclaves, mature suburbs with public transportation, and new urbanist communities will fare the best during this spurb shakeout. They will thrive because of mixed-use zoning. Instead of segregating office, commercial, and residential real estate into isolated pods, all will be merged together. Residents of these flexible communities will be able to walk to work, restaurants, and other services. If they get bored with their neighborhood, they can take the train downtown. During the spurb era, unfortunately, most of these developments couldn't be built because of zoning laws that promoted sprawl and highways.

## Highways as Teardowns

Coming to the conclusion that superhighways can be destructive to neighborhoods will be downright painful for most politicians and planners, although it's a requirement for neighborhood revival. When the

1989 San Francisco earthquake damaged the Embarcadero Freeway, the city decided to tear it down rather than rebuild it. The result was the restoration of one of the best views in the city and a 300 percent increase in adjacent property values. A similar rebound happened in Portland, Oregon, when the city removed an elevated expressway next to the Willamette River in the heart of downtown. A splendid promenade and park are there now.

In New York, development was spurred when the West Side Highway was demolished and opened up vistas of the Hudson and New Jersey. John Norquist, the former mayor of Milwaukee and president of the Congress for the New Urbanism, who constantly cites the above-mentioned examples, is one of the biggest advocates of replacing vehicle space with *people* space. He oversaw a revival of downtown Milwaukee in which a street replaced an elevated highway, triggering a $250 million increase in local property values. More than a dozen cities are considering scrapping downtown highways in attempts to revive their downtowns.

The areas that have the greatest chance of surviving in an age of contraction or high energy costs will be compact, walkable high-density communities, according to Norquist, who heads an umbrella association that represents everyone from green architects to planning firms. That means fewer, if any, superhighways ringing and bisecting cities. It's going to be a brutal battle. Zoning codes largely forbid the kind of walkable inner suburbs like Park Forest.

Except for a handful of cities—Portland, Oregon, comes to mind—laws have been written to encourage sprawl and racial and economic homogeneity and to discourage urban and infill redevelopment. The Federal Housing Administration, the government agency that has guaranteed more than 20 million mortgages (and is one component of a foreclosure bailout), even *blocked* the funding of racially integrated communities, a policy it held for decades. Even though Norquist is a progressive Democrat, who, as mayor of Milwaukee, championed the restoration of some of the city's downtrodden neighborhoods, he sees government intervention as the enemy of change. "Most of America's Main Streets would now be illegal (under current zoning codes)," Norquist, who looks like a rugged and rangy north woodsman, told me. "You would have to get [zoning variances] for them. We need to embrace urban complexity if we want an interesting life. We can save the American dream and increase productivity instead of lowering the quality of life."

## Demographic Drivers

Age dictates a different set of priorities in home and community styles over time. Once you hit fifty, traffic jams, parking lots, and tollgates get mighty old. You want and *need* the exercise to maintain your health and vigor. Getting out and seeing people on the sidewalk or just walking to get a cup of coffee becomes a subtle and cherished pleasure when you've spent most of your adult life in the suburbs sitting in cars. Those over fifty-five also want less home maintenance and may have tired long ago of mowing lawns and pulling weeds. *It's somebody else's turn*, they're saying in a growing chorus. That could explain why, when asked to describe "the most desirable living situation," they are three times more likely than a twenty-five- to thirty-four-year-old to say "a townhouse in the city." They will no longer care that much about school districts and prefer public transportation to a long drive. They will be reducing their living space, energy/carbon footprint, and garage space all at once. As they get older and retreat to a city life, their lifestyle will get greener.

Will older boomers also consider way-past-their-prime suburbs like Park Forest or down-on-their-luck, working-class inner city neighborhoods like South Chicago? I think so, especially if those areas are part of the overall demographic-driven rediscovery of urban virtues. The "move back to the city" trend is already happening in cities that have long been left for dead. Central business districts increased in population from 1990 to 2000 in St. Louis, Baltimore, Buffalo, Norfolk, Pittsburgh, Dayton, Detroit, Washington, DC, Cleveland, and Milwaukee, according to the Census Bureau. Except for maybe Washington, few of these cities would make anyone's list of glamorous places.

The preference for getting out of cars and reinhabiting core cities and suburbs is in synch with the New Urbanism mission. One of its key gauges in measuring productivity and the success of its community designs is vehicle miles traveled (VMT). If this measure of driving is lowered, people can spend more time in their community or at work. Human-scale neighborhoods enhance the lives of the residents, who can walk to stores and offices. They're also healthier. A study conducted by the U.S. Environmental Protection Agency found that urban infill sites (inner-city neighborhoods) dramatically reduced VMT and resulted in cleaner local air quality. The agency looked at sites within San Diego; Montgomery County, Maryland; and West Palm Beach, Florida.

The reduced driving requirements in each community meant from 39 percent to 52 percent fewer VMT compared to new, car-dependent developments. Smog and other air-toxin reductions ranged from 37 percent to 316 percent. More road building didn't reduce traffic in each of these cases. Expanding roads encourages more dispersed development. In other words, build the highway and more cars and pollution will follow. This is the kind of pattern the new urbanists want to reverse.

## The Worth of Walkable Communities

Norquist, who says he hasn't driven to work in more than five years, promotes the kind of mixed-use zoning that was prevalent in mature cities like Chicago, Philadelphia, and New York. Down the street from your house or apartment would be a deli, bakery, butcher, grocer, restaurant, shoe repair shop, and barber. There was no need to jump into a car, and you got exercise running your errands.

Walkability will add value to developments that support this return to viable city life. In researching his 2007 book *The Option of Urbanism: Investing in a New American Dream*, Christopher Leinberger quantified this pedestrian-friendly premium of higher real estate values for walkable communities. In 2007, condos in downtown White Plains, New York, sold for $750 a square foot—*twice* as much as home buyers were willing to pay for detached homes in car-dependent communities.

In Kirkland, Washington (near Seattle), urban condos in walkable areas were priced at $540 square foot in 2007, compared with $358 per square foot in car-locked communities. Even in the Detroit area, the birthplace of the ailing U.S. car industry, buyers were willing to pay a 40 percent premium for walkability.

Total energy consumption almost always drops in densely packed, pedestrian-friendly areas. A normal suburban household burns up about 240 million BTUs (British thermal units, a measure of combustion) yearly. Of that total, slightly more than half goes into transportation.

When a green house is built on a city lot, household energy use drops by about a factor of three. Even more savings are gained by building an energy-efficient or high-performance home that produces energy. It would be possible to see a 55 percent increase in property value over a two-year period in a green house. Although these figures are subject to a lot of variation—it depends on lifestyle and energy use—the main message is that high-density, urban green housing can be the most energy efficient.

Another key building block of the New Urbanism agenda is transit-oriented development. In the movement's charter, one item specifically calls for "transit, pedestrian, and bicycle systems that should maximize access and mobility throughout the region while reducing dependence upon the automobile." The charter also promotes patterns of development that respect "historical patterns, precedents, and boundaries."

If there's a way to get people out of their cars and into their communities, new urbanists will seize on it and implement it in their plans. You can see their intentional design at work in places like the Kentlands, outside of Washington, DC, or Bigelow's HomeTown, which Norquist admires. Although the more than two hundred new urbanist communities often look like well-scrubbed retreads of traditional communities, everything in these areas has been redesigned, from how storm water is managed to the width of streets.

## Better Land-Use Planning

Wise land-use planning means using nearly every resource efficiently. Connecting to green infrastructure such as watersheds is also part of the plan, which creates "greenways" that take into account wildlife migration patterns, natural stream flows, wetlands, and the original topography. In the new urbanist conservation community that I live in (Prairie Crossing in Grayslake, Illinois), for example, extensive mapping of storm-water flow into wetlands and a man-made lake was done before any home was built. The water flows into an existing creek on its way to the Des Plaines River, a tributary of the Illinois and Mississippi rivers. I can trace the water rolling off my roof all the way to St. Louis and the Gulf of Mexico.

Andres Duany and Elizabeth Plater-Zyberk, the husband-and-wife team who run an influential New Urbanism planning firm in Miami—the Microsoft of urban planning companies—designed communities like the Kentlands in Maryland and Seaside in northern Florida to make suburban growth sustainable. Like many new urbanist communities, homes in their developments cost up to $40,000 more than conventional subdivisions. Their designs incorporate small but important details like porches on every home, narrow streets, and mini-downtowns where you can shop and eat out without driving.

Sidewalks that connect with retail areas are essential in the New Urbanism worldview. Duany and Plater-Zyberk argue that a misconception pervades suburban life that highways are "free goods," that is, they don't have a perceived cost so they're used excessively, in a manner I call the "buffet effect." Duany and Plater-Zyberk estimate that subsidizing vehicle space with government funds amounts to $700 billion in economic inefficiencies. Spurbs needlessly layer on these expenses, and that translates into wasting a lot of productive time simply driving around. Somebody else ends up paying for medical care from accidents, bad air, and the ill health resulting from the car culture, the conventional wisdom goes. That *somebody* is everyone.

## There Will Be Blood

Like Norquist, Duany and his wife have fought numerous battles over zoning codes that mandate single-family homes and single-use areas. Many of these ordinances sprang from the government's subsidization of suburbs and the interstate highway system after World War II through programs like the Veterans Administration (VA) and the Federal Housing Administration (FHA). Government-backed loans became cheaper than paying rent, and urban areas became patchworks of Levittowns. "Intentionally or not, the FHA and VA programs discouraged the renovation of existing housing stock, while turning their back on the construction of row houses, mixed-use buildings, and other urban housing types," they write in their 2000 polemic *Suburban Nation: The Rise of Sprawl and the Decline of the American Dream.*

There is no lack of prime examples in nearly every metropolitan area for new urbanist models. Duany says he has admired the core areas of Lake Forest, Illinois; Marymount, Ohio; Coral Gables, Florida; Cleveland Heights, Ohio; Forest Hills, New York; and Riverside, Illinois. Yet following the new urbanist script is not enough. More attention needs to be paid to making every housing unit energy and resource efficient,

# Buying Local

All intelligent urban planning is local. To succeed, the de-spurbing of America will have to go beyond rebuilding inner suburbs and cities. It will need to revitalize entire regional economies. That doesn't amount to creating walkable, mini–shopping districts with the same old national chain stores. It translates into buying locally from merchants who live in the area. Family farms and farmers' markets are perfect examples of how this works. They bring their products into areas and sell directly. They support local employment, add to the local tax base, and reduce the costs of transporting food. Since most produce travels at least one thousand miles to reach a supermarket (from California, Florida, and Washington), obtaining produce locally reduces the pollution created by transportation (trucks, trains, etc.). Less fossil fuel is burned and less carbon dioxide goes into the atmosphere.

Buying local makes ecological sense as well. Irreplaceable fertile farmland is used productively and not plowed under for another parking lot, subdivision, or megamall. Local food is fresher and tastes better. The downward trend in the number of family farms—nearly 5 million lost since 1935—is curbed by buying local. A growing movement called "Community Supported Agriculture" takes this one step further. A network of farms provides organized cooperatives or individuals with fresh farm goods on a subscription basis. In the Midwest, according to FamilyFarmed.org, an entire farming region from Minnesota to Indiana is supported by these groups. Many of these agricultural entrepreneurs specialize in premium-priced organic products, from bakery goods to dairy items.

Locally owned businesses bolster neighborhoods more than chain stores do. According to one study by the Institute for Local Self-Reliance, three times as much money stays in the local economy when consumers buy from neighborhood businesses instead of large chains. When city and regional planners eye the next shopping mall with its massive infrastructure and energy costs, they can't forget that local business people live and work locally, pay taxes, and have a vested interest in bolstering their neighborhood. These producers' bottom line is aligned with the community's interest most of the time.

but such efficiency is not necessarily emphasized in the design of the new urbanist homes.

Simply having public transportation in the area isn't enough to end the cul-de-sac syndrome. It needs to be accessible. Both Portland, Oregon, and Miami, Duany points out, have light-rail systems and have encouraged high-density building in their downtowns. But most people drive in Miami, which he says is "bigger and poorer" and doesn't have the easy access or acceptance of public transportation that Portland has. "In Portland," Plater-Zyberk adds, "everyone is on the same page."

Although reducing vehicular traffic is one approach among many in the "de-spurbing" of America, it will be a long and protracted battle against the inherited Jeffersonian wisdom that vehicle mobility directly equates with individual freedom. High energy prices started to change this entitlement thinking before a recession drove gasoline costs down in late 2008. Sport-utility vehicle sales collapsed in that year after having peaked in 2005, and public transportation ridership was climbing. Leinberger calls this "the beginning of the end of sprawl."

No matter what happens to energy prices, it's clear that excessive use of carbon-based fuels is bad for human health and the environment in addition to being highly inefficient. We've already paid dearly for the ever-worsening spurb lifestyle. It's time to reverse course. "The present relationship between cities and automobiles represents, in short, one of those jokes that history sometimes plays on progress," wrote Jane Jacobs in her classic *The Death and Life of Great American Cities* more than forty years ago.

There can be a successful fusion of New Urbanism and a sensible response to energy efficiency, environmental sensitivity, and affordability. In my efforts to discover emerging communities that could become economical and ecodynamic models for the future, I found a mother lode in two areas that are low-profile areas for real-estate development: Wisconsin and Tennessee.

# CHAPTER 11

# The Bill Comes Due
## Which Places Will Prosper?

I AM SAVORING the vista from one last hill from which I can enjoy the lush green curves of the valley that entranced Frank Lloyd Wright. This promontory is in Spring Green, Wisconsin, where Wright built his Monticello: Taliesin East. The word means "shining brow" and is the name of a Welsh poet. The expansive 30,000-square-foot home embodies nearly every virtue, eccentricity, and tragedy his genius brought into the world. His mistress, her two children, and four others were murdered here in 1914 by an insane employee who set fire to the house and attacked with an axe those trying to escape.

The house burned again in 1925, and, like Jefferson, Wright spent most of his adult life (some fifty years) rebuilding and remodeling it while deeply in debt. Because the house depended on fireplaces for heat in the unforgiving Wisconsin winter, he often decamped to his Taliesin West near Scottsdale, Arizona, during the coldest months. His Wisconsin home has elements of all of his most famous homes and takes advantage of the views of the verdant, undulating hills from generous windows, a catwalk, and towers. A gracious blend of intimate and dramatic spaces, it combines serene courtyards with native limestone to create a sense that the hill itself *created* the house.

While Taliesin East embodies so much of modern architecture and of Wright's boundless creative spirit, it's rarely recognized as perhaps the birthplace of the idealized Jeffersonian suburb and an incubator for some of the antidotes to it. Gazing over the valleys of the area of Wisconsin that the glaciers spared, I attempt to channel Wright's vision of an ideally built environment that is affordable and sustainable

Frank Lloyd Wright's Taliesin home in Spring Green, Wisconsin
*Credit:* John Wasik

(Taliesin is a poor example of this concept). What matters most is what Wright never really built, the product of his imagination that symbolically launched tens of thousands of tract developments.

When I first saw the 12-by-12-foot wooden Broadacre model at Taliesin, it looked oddly familiar. It was suburbia writ large with up-to-five-acre lots, except it wasn't dominated by estate houses. First presented in 1935 and conceived at a time when Wright had virtually no clients, the intriguing model lays out his tableau for Usonian homes, which Wright said could be built by their owners for $5,000. Nevertheless, homebuilders were influenced by his Broadacre/Usonian philosophy. His Usonian homes challenged the orthodoxy of balloon-frame construction with an aesthetically pleasing home for the masses that he hoped would be affordable.

Wright saw Broadacre as the answer to centralized cities and the antidote to cold, massive Le Corbusier–like conglomerations of high rises. The individual and not the state would dominate in Wright's slap at Communist thinking. The spirit of Jefferson and Emerson would reign in each owner's one- to five-acre lots, integration with working farms, and graceful highways that would connect the Usonian family to the rest of the world through their automobiles. Wright believed that every Usonian citizen would desire to be his own farmer, mechanic, homebuilder, and participant in a working democracy. At a time when the entire U.S. population could have fit into Texas and was suffering from the Great Depression, Wright saw Broadacre as a plan to liberate people from cities, evil banks (he proposed a new monetary system), and a population density of more than fifteen people per acre.

The Usonian vision built upon Locke, Jefferson, and the agrarian democrats. Land gave you power and purpose. "When every man, woman, and child may be born to put his feet on his own acres and every unborn child finds his acre waiting for him when he is born—then democracy will have been realized," Wright wrote in *The Living City*.

The most enlightened "conservation" communities today actually preserve agrarian vistas and open space, many with working farms within them. Although Wright called urban congestion "monstrous," he may not have fathomed that his model, multiplied by a hundred thousand cloned subdivisions, would generate sprawl. He may have seen, though, that decentralization would present a better economic model for development. Part of that promise has already come true with telecommuters using Web-based tools to work from anywhere in "brain burbs."

## Machine-Driven Living

A persistent theme in Wright's meandering writings is the role of machines in architecture and society. Le Corbusier saw houses as "machines for living." Wright saw the machine in all of its forms as a way of enabling people to reach their full creative potential. His contemporary and friend social critic Lewis Mumford took a different view when he observed, "We have attempted to live off machinery and the host has devoured us." By making the automobile the principal means of exploiting freedom, Wright saw his Broadacre car community as a means of fulfilling his democratic ideal. More than any other architect, Wright achieved what Mumford called "a synthesis of nature, the machine and human activities and purposes." Broadacre City, which morphed into so many ex-urban "edge" cities, isolated office parks on expressway interchanges, and spurs (without the farms), stood for "an overcompensated protest against the reckless and indiscriminate congestion of the metropolis," Mumford noted. New Urbanist developers who have integrated farms within subdivisions (my neighborhood Prairie Crossing is one such example) also owe a debt to Wright.

While Broadacre City was never built, the philosophy of the Usonian home within it triumphed in nearly every middle-class subdivision of the twentieth and twenty-first centuries. The houses were relatively cheap and simple, used commonly available materials, and could be built on a large scale. What Wright conceived in the 1930s as a home for Everyman, eventually became the ubiquitous ranch home in hundreds of variations.

In a handful of his designs, Wright even dabbled with energy efficiency. One of his Usonian designs of that period—the Solar Hemicycle—was a passive solar model that was oriented toward the sun and heated some of the interior space through curved window walls. Also known as the Jacobs House II, the roof leaked and the house couldn't be heated adequately the way Wright designed it; nevertheless, the hemicycle was one of the first passive solar homes built in the twentieth century by a major architect. The closest Wright got to Broadacre City was Usonia, a community near Pleasantville, New York, where forty-seven homes were built on a ninety-seven-acre tract of rolling, sylvan land about an hour north of New York City. The development was started in 1948 and was followed by two other small Usonian communities.

## The Ecodynamic Community

The indirect heirs to Wright's democratic and organic philosophy are the New Urbanists, who are seeking to preserve indigenous architectural forms while making their communities work with natural elements. I didn't have to go far from Wright's home base to find an example of the evolution of those ideas. About thirty minutes east, in Middleton, Wisconsin, houses in the New Urbanist community of Middleton Hills not only mimic some of Wright's smaller Prairie-style homes, they also embrace the landscape unlike the houses in most subdivisions. Originally developed by the company founded by Wright collaborator Marshall Erdman, Middleton Hills isn't exactly Usonia; it's an upscale eco-development that has been designed around wetlands.

Designed and master planned by Andres Duany and Elizabeth Plater-Zyberk, the development aspires to spur its residents to "rediscover the sense of community that was lost during the '80s and '90s in the sprawl of isolated housing tracts, shopping developments, and office parks." Although the community doesn't connect with the charming business district of old Middleton, it has retail space at the entrance of the subdivision for small shops and restaurants.

How is the sense of community rediscovered? About four hundred single-family homes, townhouses, and live and work units are part of a design that encourages residents to walk around. The houses have small front yards, porches, and views of forty acres of green space. The streets are narrow and on a grid, permitting better traffic flow but not speed-through driving. Although there's no particular emphasis on affordability, there is a variety of price points. Downtown Madison (the state's capital) is only a few miles away, and homeowners can get there by bus.

When I visited, Middleton Hills was a curious work in progress. It was similar to many of Wright's Usonian projects—elegantly conceived yet not quite fluid in a real world that demands accessibility, aggressive energy conservation, and affordability. Like most New Urbanist communities, it's lovely to look at, but I wonder how this model will survive if it doesn't work to lower or stabilize living costs over time.

Between the time I first visited Middleton in 2007 and my return to Madison for a real estate seminar at the University of Wisconsin about a year later, the price of oil had risen 50 percent and gasoline prices had soared. People were abandoning their cars for mass transit, and the cost of food was skyrocketing due to commodity inflation and the growing of corn for ethanol fuel. If there was a place where positive social change was likely to occur, the Madison area, informed by a progressive spirit seeded by Robert La Follette in the early twentieth century, still had much to offer.

On the east side of Madison, I found Veridian Homes' Grandview Commons development, built on a hill overlooking Interstate 94 and possessing a stunning view of the Wisconsin State Capitol dome. In keeping with its New Urbanist cousin Middleton Hills, the 230-acre Grandview reflects traditional Midwestern home styles, and has narrow streets and porches. Where it exceeds the reach of the standard New Urbanist model is in energy efficiency. All of the company's new homes are built to Wisconsin Energy Star and Green Built Home standards. That means every house has energy-efficient appliances and heating and cooling systems that can be twice as efficient as those used in conventional homes. And here's the economic pitch missing from far too many green homes that I've seen: a higher projected resale value.

Veridian's commitment to energy was buried in a raft of other considerations such as land planning, habitat restoration, water conservation, and the need to "restore harmony between communities and their environments." Most of what the developer had promised in terms of walkable amenities, such as 150,000 square feet of retail space in a town center and a city library, hadn't been built when I visited. Yet the promise of the place created an unsatisfied longing for something more complete, more organic in its search for sustainability.

More important, the Veridian development philosophy undermines the suburban obsession for large lots and homes in a number of ways. David Simon, the president of Veridian, told me, "Two-thirds of what we build is higher density. We started with building on smaller lots. We use land more efficiently and it lowers infrastructure costs." Simon also shrunk lot sizes due to the rising cost of land, which used to account for 25 percent of a home's cost, but now can exceed 30 percent. Although this is a move in the right direction, even more needs to be done to address energy concerns.

## The Community: Producing Power and Preserving Resources

New Urbanism embodies the ideas that are needed for a transition to energy-independent communities. But what if a developer created a master-planned community that could provide most of its own power? What if municipalities started to pay *every* homeowner to install solar and other energy-generating improvements? It would be a smart public-policy decision for local government and a savvy financial move for property owners.

Berkeley, California, for example, has offered to pay for the up-front costs of solar installations and expects to recoup those costs in higher assessed values (and property taxes) over twenty years. The emerging concept is that energy efficiency not only addresses sustainability, energy prices, and climate change, it *adds value*. Until that's the dominant message from government and private developers, American homebuilding will remain mired in its nineteenth-century mode of operation.

The potential for energy features to enhance property values could be one of the industry's most powerful selling points after the bust. I found it in South Chicago in one of the city's poorest neighborhoods. It was in evidence north of San Diego, where the Del Sur development is eventually going to encompass more than three thousand homes, 20 percent of which may have solar panels.

Developer Fred Maas has used his mass-purchasing power combined with generous state subsidies to bring down the cost of solar systems, which retailed for $24,000 apiece before rebates and discounts. More than 450 of the homes were to be priced for low- and moderate-income residents. In this part of the country, you could've easily paid $850,000 for a 2,000-square-foot ranch at the height of the boom and have little else to show for your investment. By adhering to conservation principles, developers can build value for homeowners as well as save on development costs—savings they can pass along in the form of lower home prices.

What about simply not building on every available parcel and conserving open land instead? A study by Applied Ecological Services, a design firm in Brodhead, Wisconsin, concludes that communities that conserve land can be 15 percent to 54 percent cheaper to build than conventional subdivisions. Savings per lot range from $5,000 to $70,000, based on narrowing roadways and scaling back storm sewers (and building swales). Even the sacred American lawn can be downsized to reduce water use and runoff. Eliminating a storm sewer and retaining local water in a natural system such as a wetland can save up to $1 million.

## Conservation and the Future of Communities

Conservation is an economically essential element in communities where resources are scarce. In Civano, a community in Tucson, Arizona, green homes with rainwater harvesting systems can save up to 58 percent on potable water consumption, which is critical in the middle of the Sonoran Desert. The homes also use 32 percent less energy for heating and cooling than conventional homes do.

Although it's not unusual to see developers increasingly using solar panels in the Southwest, few have truly integrated the energy-producing technology with total-resource-conservation approaches such as gray-water reuse for irrigation or site planning that minimizes disruption (local building codes can be an impediment). Only a handful of developers are synthesizing energy- and resource-conservation measures with new urbanist concepts to build communities of green homes.

During the course of my research, I came across only one project in the United States that exemplified a comprehensive energy conservation and cultural community. Emerging from the design plans of a nexus of U.S. Department of Energy (DOE) engineers and architects in the lush green valleys of the western Cumberland Mountains is Walden Reserve, Tennessee. About forty miles from the Oak Ridge National Laboratory, a hotbed for federal energy research near Knoxville, it's designed to host some twenty thousand residents. It is one of the continent's first "deep green" communities that's starting from scratch in creating zero-energy homes that produce more power than they consume.

The self-contained community—built on six thousand wooded acres—will not only feature homes with solar panels and tight insulation, but its own water, cogeneration, biodigesting, and photovoltaic systems. If everything goes as planned, at some point it will produce enough power to sell back to the local utility, the Tennessee Valley Authority. It's being designed by DOE engineers like Jeff Christian, a University of Wisconsin graduate who's been interested in energy since the 1970s.

Christian has built a few zero-energy homes for Habitat for Humanity nearby in Lenoir City. When I visited him in Knoxville—the site of the 1980 World's Fair (where energy was the theme)—Christian said zero-energy homes can be operated for an energy budget of 50 cents a day. "People respond to the idea. They just need education."

*Zero-energy* is a snappy and overly ambitious phrase for selling homes, but it heads down the path of making each home less dependent on outside resources and power. Guidelines for the evolving home standards are being provided to builders by the Leadership in Energy and Environmental Design (LEED), Energy Star, and a program of the National Association of Home Builders.

Entire cities, such as New Orleans, have employed green standards. The town of Greensburg, Kansas, which is rebuilding after a devastating tornado, requires that all buildings qualify for LEED platinum status, the highest level. Green building will become more than a chic marketing pitch as builders realize how to brand their developments and communicate the economic value of saving energy and resources. Green homes will be huge cost savers for owners over time.

Costs per unit for green homes will come down as energy appliances are mass-produced and installed as standard features in large subdivisions and city infill projects. The missing piece is how the new energy reality will change the culture of development: Will it simply offer ownership savings or is a much larger, organic change afoot? What will happen to spurbs? I predict many of them will turn into ghost towns.

"With baby boomers downsizing and echo boomers looking to be near the action, the market [for single-family homes on large lots on the ex-urban edge] will be saturated for years," says New Urbanist John Norquist. "The market for townhouses and condos in walkable, mixed-used neighborhoods hasn't been hit nearly as hard [in the housing bust] and will come back much faster."

Will these new ideas in real estate development and home design bring us closer together and sustain human-scale communities? New Urbanism is, in the view of sociologist Robert Putnam, "an ongoing experiment to see whether our community life outweighs our hunger for private backyards, discount megamalls, and easy parking. In the end, Americans will get largely the kind of physical space we demand; if we don't really want more community, we won't get it."

## Poised for Recovery—or Not

If there's a way of predicting what will happen to the U.S. housing market by 2015, the past provides a prologue. Areas where subprime mortgages dominated, resulting in higher-than-average bankruptcy and foreclosure rates, may take years to recover. The economic principle is simple: A huge supply of homes will eventually be absorbed by new buyers. Every foreclosed house will be sold at a steep discount relative to its former market value and will depress the prices in every neighborhood where that's a problem. Why would you buy a house at full retail when the house next to you is being sold at 30 percent to 60 percent off? The bubble inflated those market values to begin with, so these areas will see price reductions of up to 50 percent before the housing recovery is in full swing.

Also important are population, demographics, and job growth. Lost local jobs are the leading negative factor for home prices. That situation bodes poorly for manufacturing regions that have lost jobs to Asia and Mexico. Buyers can surely find bargain-priced homes in these areas, but they shouldn't expect any appreciation. They may even lose equity.

Although there are a few exceptions, the heart of America's old manufacturing core in Ohio, Indiana, Illinois, Michigan, Wisconsin, Minnesota, and Pennsylvania will continue to suffer. The bright spot is that Americans are still relatively mobile—if they're able to sell their homes. Then they can move where the jobs are or where housing is cheaper. No doubt the baby boomers and their children may still find the Sunbelt attractive. That doesn't mean, however, that home prices in Arizona, California, Georgia, Nevada, and coastal areas will continue to grow as they did. There may be continued price declines as the market recovers from bankruptcies and foreclosures and prices fall back down to pre-2005 levels. Most of what I'm describing is simple supply-and-demand economics, which was largely forgotten during the boom.

Now comes the interesting part. A notable shift from the overpriced regions to less-expensive areas began well before the boom. West Coast residents found greater values in the Rocky Mountain states, fueling growth in Colorado, Montana, Utah, and western Wyoming. Those who could telecommute found that they could get much more for their money, with splendid vistas and recreation, in Ogden, Utah; Wenatchee, Washington; or Boulder, Colorado, than in Silicon Valley or the Seattle suburbs. Boston- and New York–area residents found they could live much better and buy more real estate in Charlotte, North Carolina, or Atlanta's suburbs. These highly networked employees migrated to "brain burbs," such as Boulder, or any place that gave them high-bandwidth Internet access. This trend will continue as the hotbeds for technology innovation, such as Boston, Seattle, and the San Francisco Bay Area, stay pricey. Along with New York, these innovation centers will likely remain desirable as cultural and intellectual capitals. It will still be expensive to live there because they will remain "glamour cities," in the opinion of Yale economist Robert Shiller.

## Still Room for Growth

The price and migration patterns I've studied for the better part of a decade indicate that the long-term growth that most sprawling cities have experienced will likely contract during an extended recovery period. But suburban areas where car commutes are long or arduous are candidates for the most severe contraction. That pattern will constrict growth in greater Los Angeles, San Diego, San Francisco, Denver, Houston, Chicago, St. Louis, Atlanta, New York, Washington, DC, and Boston.

This long-term growth picture includes a few exceptions and contradictions. Cities or suburbs with a combination of cultural amenities, health care, educational institutions, and neighborhoods with "ped-ex" zones (that is, having high walkability, trails, and bike lanes) will prosper long term. Typically, these urban or suburban enclaves offer theaters, shopping, dining, community centers, and mixed-use zoning in what urban scholar Joel Kotkin calls "the new localism." This old urbanist trend will favor established cities like Austin, New York, Boston, Philadelphia, Chicago, Kansas City, Denver, San Francisco, Seattle, and Portland, Oregon. Although those cities will suffer short-term price declines, over time they may move back to the historical average of home price appreciation, which is around 2.5 percent to 3 percent annually, or roughly the same as per capita income growth. So the cities that are expensive now may remain dear for the very reason that they offer so much through their mature neighborhoods, where an increasing number of aging Americans may prefer to live when they become empty nesters.

Another positive growth factor is that built-in institutions are unlikely to be uprooted by economic downturns. Universities, museums, hospitals, and cultural institutions will largely survive the housing bust. Don't count out cultural and human capital corridors like Boston; New York–New Jersey–Connecticut; Pittsburgh; Philadelphia; Research Triangle (North Carolina); the Texas Triangle (Austin-Houston-Dallas–Fort Worth-San Antonio); San Francisco Bay Area; Puget Sound (Seattle-Tacoma); Wasatch Valley (Salt Lake City–Provo); Denver-Boulder; Gainesville, Florida; and Chicago-Milwaukee-Madison. These areas are also blessed by large research institutions, which attract investment capital, knowledge workers, and new real estate activity over time.

In the worst-case scenario—that is, if high energy prices return and persist—the spurbing of America will most likely crash to a halt. That will mostly endanger growth in sprawling "boomburbs" such as Gilbert, Arizona; Henderson, Nevada; Irvine, California; Arlington, Texas; Coral Springs, Florida; Lakewood, Colorado; and Bellevue, Washington. It's unfair to lump all of these towns into one pot, but if high energy prices prevail or job growth declines, the median growth of 181 percent for these places, accounting for an influx of almost 6 million people (through 2006 when the boom peaked), can't continue at that pace. That still leaves scores of midsize to small cities that are poised for expansion if they're favored with job and population growth. Another negative factor for spurbs would be any changes in development laws and the U.S. tax code. Take away the multiple real estate tax breaks for the spurbing of America and ex-urban sprawl will abate. A paucity of institutional credit and long-term contraction of commercial building is also something to watch.

The economically oriented migration out of the highest-priced housing and tax zones will benefit areas that were bypassed by the boom. Overall, demographic trends still favor migration from the Midwest and Northeast to Sunbelt states. Retirees from Illinois, Michigan, Ohio, and Minnesota will still favor Arizona, Nevada, Florida, and Texas. The warmer states also have economic appeal because of lower taxes and cost of living.

## The Watch List

In preparing the list that follows, I carefully analyzed information from a number of public and private research sources. I used data from the Federal Reserve to pinpoint the worst trouble spots, or as the Fed called it, "heat maps" of areas where foreclosures, subprime mortgages, speculation, and job losses were highest. I also tracked home prices using data from the Office of Federal Housing Enterprise Oversight house price index, the S&P/Case-Shiller home price indexes, the National Association of Realtors, the Census Bureau, and the *Wall Street Journal*.

The list concerns those areas most likely to experience further declines or a prolonged recovery. People will certainly move to and live in these areas; just don't expect any price appreciation for several years. More pain may be in the works, and recovery is highly dependent on how the Obama administration's bailout works over time. The last three lists include places that have been appreciating at below-average rates. Although I can't say for sure which places will be guaranteed to grow, the risk of losing equity will be much lower in those places, and buyers will get much more for their housing dollars. These areas would also be worth considering for relocation or retirement.

## Most Troubled Areas

These areas may experience the longest recovery period:

➤ Inland Empire, California (Riverside, San Bernardino)
➤ Sacramento, Stockton, Lodi, Merced, and Modesto, California
➤ Desert corridor (Las Vegas, Nevada and Phoenix, Arizona areas)
➤ Southwest Florida (Fort Myers, Naples, Sarasota)
➤ Miami-Dade, Florida
➤ Detroit (southeastern Michigan)
➤ Cleveland (and industrial cities throughout Ohio)
➤ San Diego, California

## Less-Troubled Areas

In these areas, price declines will be offset in a shorter period by growth in jobs and population:

➤ Atlanta, Columbus, Georgia
➤ Denver, Colorado
➤ Baltimore, Maryland–Washington, DC corridor
➤ Los Angeles County, California
➤ Tampa–St. Petersburg, Florida
➤ Orlando, Lakeland, Florida
➤ Chicago area, Illinois

## Bargain Cities

In these areas, housing prices will be lower relative to major adjacent population areas:

➤ Charlotte, North Carolina
➤ Raleigh-Durham (Research Triangle), North Carolina
➤ Baton Rouge, Louisiana
➤ Chattanooga, Tennessee

➤ Colorado Springs, Colorado
➤ El Paso, Texas
➤ Eugene-Springfield, Oregon
➤ Davenport, Iowa
➤ Rock Island and Rockford, Illinois (Quad Cities)
➤ Dover, Delaware
➤ Louisville and Lexington, Kentucky
➤ Gulfport-Biloxi, Mississippi
➤ Gainesville and Ocala, Florida
➤ Oklahoma City and Tulsa, Oklahoma
➤ Richmond, Virginia
➤ Wichita, Kansas
➤ Spokane and Yakima, Washington

## Surprise Cities

These cities are primed for some growth and offer multiple amenities:

➤ Austin, San Antonio, and Dallas–Fort Worth, Texas
➤ Salt Lake City and Ogden-Provo, Utah
➤ Pittsburgh and Philadelphia, Pennsylvania
➤ Birmingham, Alabama
➤ Lexington, Kentucky
➤ Des Moines, Iowa
➤ Minneapolis–St. Paul, Minnesota
➤ Kansas City and St. Louis, Missouri

## Off-the-Radar Cities

These small, desirable cities experienced below-average growth (2001–2007) and may be even better bargains:

➤ Auburn, Alabama
➤ College Station, Texas
➤ Dalton, Georgia
➤ Greenville, North Carolina
➤ Jonesboro, Arkansas
➤ Muncie, Indiana

➤ Parkersburg, West Virginia
➤ Sandusky, Ohio
➤ Sumter, South Carolina
➤ Yuma, Arizona

## Revitalizing the American Dream

What will enable a metropolitan area to grow in an age of expensive energy, rising taxes, constrained resources, and an aging population? Leading thinkers, research organizations, and environmental groups offer a host of approaches. Here are some of the most compelling.

**Unlink property taxes from school funding and local development.** The key is to provide diversified school and infrastructure funding—from local, regional, state, and federal sources. This will help keep families from moving ever farther away from central cities to find better schools and housing values. Educational quality simply needs to improve in *every* school district if America is to stay in the global economic game. "The problem with U.S. education is a problem of inequality," says Fareed Zakaria, a skilled observer of geopolitics. "This will, over time, translate into a competitiveness problem, because if the United States can't educate and train a third of the working population to compete in a knowledge economy, this will drag down the country." That means providing even more federal funding to local schools and mixing sources of tax revenue from state and local taxation.

**Prioritize transportation funding.** Channel the majority of federal transportation subsidies into public transportation and road and infrastructure repairs. Rebuild the bridges, overpasses, grade crossings, and roads we have now. Direct a greater proportion of federal dollars into urban light rail, zero-emission buses, trails, public transit, bike paths, and intercity high-speed trains. Provide funding to new communities that emphasize grid layouts to minimize street traffic. Minimize the building of high-speed, multilane highways. Provide tax incentives and financing for developments that are within walking distance of public transportation. Much of this has been proposed and will be funded by the Obama administration and Congress, although regional, state, and local governments also need to plan, fund, and accommodate the need for more diversified public transportation options. Interstate and intrastate high-speed rail will also reduce the need for highway building and reduce carbon dioxide production.

**Create model zoning codes.** This can be done on the local, county, and state levels. Allow for mixed-use zoning that encourages pedestrian and bike traffic and discourages sprawl while promoting green buffer zones. Model ordinances should be written for areas that want to create livable, walkable, and bikeable communities.

**Update building codes for the twenty-first century.** Require that all new construction and communities be mandated to meet the standards set forth in the LEED, Energy Star, or other local programs. Montgomery County, Maryland, for example, is requiring that new homes meet Energy Star guidelines. Mandate water conservation measures in home and subdivision design. A national energy building code needs to require conservation for every new or remodeled building. On a local level, building permit fees can be reduced for green improvements. The City of Chicago, for example, will waive up to $25,000 in fees for green rehabs, depending upon the level of improvements.

**Create green jobs, particularly in blighted areas.** Millions of jobs can be created for refurbishing substandard housing, installing energy appliances, building public transportation, and retrofitting buildings. According to the Apollo Alliance, for every $1 billion invested in public transportation, 47,500 jobs are supported. Wind power creates 2.77 jobs per megawatt produced; solar photovoltaic manufacturers generate 7.254 jobs. A comprehensive energy program should mandate that all new buildings follow national efficiency guidelines and should provide as much funding as was invested in the space race of the 1960s to carbon-neutral energy technologies. A tax on carbon emissions at every level—industrial, commercial, and residential—would finance this research and development. In addition, take away the $47 billion in subsidies to the oil and coal industries and invest it in clean-energy and building research and in tax credits. Although the Obama administration is fully committed to a green jobs program, it needs to couple that effort with a carbon tax on large, private vehicles over a certain weight limit and on buildings that don't meet improved environmental standards. An increase in the federal gasoline tax is another option.

**Trim real estate tax breaks.** Write-offs for mortgage interest, property taxes, and capital gains distort and artificially inflate home prices. They effectively provide subsidies for those in the most expensive areas, ranging from $26,285 per owner-occupied unit in the San Francisco Bay Area to $12,759 in Hawaii, according to a University of Pennsylvania Wharton School study. Start with repealing the mortgage-interest deduction. Desirable areas would still be in demand if these tax breaks go away, and prices may fall in others. That will enhance affordability. Offer tax breaks for builders and owners who reduce the cost of ownership through environmental or urban planning improvements. If developers want to build new shopping areas, for example, offer them tax credits for building green, providing bike and walking trails, and reducing water consumption.

**Fund a smart grid.** Provide the necessary funding to update the electrical grid for this century (the initial 2009 stimulus plan isn't enough). Ideally, the grid should be able to respond automatically to power surges without breakdowns. Supplement the grid with substantial investments in clean energy and modern electrical storage. Mandate that utilities provide services to tell customers when off-peak power is available and provide tax incentives for homeowners who want to create their own clean power supplies. Require net metering and buyback of home-generated electricity. Enhance the tax credit package to a twenty-year horizon for those who want to invest in clean energy production. Decouple utility industry profits from sales through tax credits. Reverse the business model: The less power they sell through energy-conservation measures, the *more* money they can make.

**Create private incentives for more affordable housing.** Mandate that new developments offer a variety of housing by size and price, including rentals and high-density townhomes. For every $1,000 that home prices rise, 217,000 families are priced out of purchase. Offer builders tax breaks for keeping homes under 3,000 square feet and increasing density. Create programs that will lower closing costs. Make clear disclosure of mortgage document details a priority. Show worst-case scenarios on rate increases for adjustable loans and detail all possible costs. Not everyone should own a home, so the government should provide a better way of supporting renters.

**Provide personalized, national health care.** American mobility is largely based on employment. Millions want not only a better job with higher wages but also freedom from catastrophic health expenses. The only way to achieve that is to delink health coverage from employment (and the tax breaks provided to employers for offering health care). In a personalized, universal program, the government can contract with private companies who bid for the business to underwrite policies that cover the entire country. This will enable people to be more productive, take any kind of employment, and move wherever they want. It will indirectly help housing because Americans won't be locked into communities. They may be able to move to less-populous areas and telecommute. A guaranteed universal savings plan for all Americans is also essential.

## Good Ecology Makes Economic Sense

As ever more people move into U.S. metropolitan areas, it's possible to embrace progressive change without sacrificing economic growth. The suburbs, where more than half of Americans now live, will continue to prosper if they adopt some of the sustainable living patterns of the best urban neighborhoods. More than 140 million people are projected to live in the suburbs in 2020, outnumbering city dwellers by 92 million. Cul-de-sac zones don't have to be dead ends, but to move on, we have to realize the punishing limitations of nineteenth- and twentieth-century building and planning.

Yet this growth must take into account harsh new realities in water, energy, and land use. Americans may begin downsizing their mega developments, big-box stores, and spurbs, even as Chinese and Indians and just about anyone with means in a developing country will be going in the opposite direction in their quest to have what Americans have— or *had*. About one thousand new cars a day are added to the roads of Beijing. China will have more cars than the United States in 2025, if not sooner. Their break-neck urbanization will cost dearly in terms of poorer air quality, depleted watersheds and mineral resources, and more carbon dioxide to further warm the planet. Their emulation and adoption of our profligate lifestyle imperils us all. Western countries need no longer be the bad examples of unsustainable consumption.

It's a far better proposition for the human race that we provide a comprehensive set of sustainable technologies and demand that they be put into place. The housing crisis has seeded an immense opportunity for change. Prosperity can be shared globally, but to do that, we have to tap into that most infinite of resources—our imaginations.

# Epilogue
## Cleaning Up, Moving On

THE AMERICAN HOME BUST cascaded through the global economy, triggering recessions in North America and Europe. Even emerging stock markets were hurt by its impact on global finance. China experienced a broad-based slowdown. Seized by the widespread economic malaise, 53 percent of American voters ushered one-term Senator Barack Obama into the presidency.

By the end of 2008, the losses from mortgage securities alone cost banks, insurers, and other lenders more than $1 trillion. Collateral damage included a $6 trillion crash in global stock market prices while foreclosures continued unabated. Not only were the U.S. housing market and general economy in shambles, retirement plans like 401(k)s were down as much as 40 percent. Unless Congress's and regulators' remedial actions take hold in a dramatic way, some 8 million are expected to lose their homes between 2008 and 2011 and even more may lose the lion's share of their life savings.

What happened to the last nest eggs of American savings? Nearly nine out of ten homes in some areas around Las Vegas had mortgage balances that exceeded home values and almost eight out of ten in Fort Myers, Florida, and Riverside County, California. Entire subdivisions and towns from central California to Miami became foreclosure gulches where homeowners were either thrown out of their homes or simply walked away. Was this the end of a long cycle of American prosperity and mobility or simply the mother of all corrections after three asset bubbles exploded? "The pain of this reverse movement," wrote Robert

Shiller in the *New York Times,* "could leave a psychological scar that will be with all of us for the rest of our lives."

More important, the cultural impact of not being able to sell a home, count on its wealth-building potential, or even reap its full value in a depressed market is profound. Combined with rising inflation and food prices, more than 40 percent of those on food stamps were coming from *working* families in late 2008, up from 30 percent a decade earlier. Loan officers, mortgage brokers, construction workers, real estate appraisers, and agents long ago joined the growing ranks of the unemployed, accounting for a 20 percent increase in demand at food banks. Record numbers of Americans couldn't pay their home-energy bills.

Beth and Fabrizio Faieta, the couple in Florida (introduced in Chapter 1) who hoped to build a nest egg with their investment homes, obtained some relief by selling one of their houses for $325,000, although the mortgage on it was $420,000. The bank foreclosed on their duplex, and they were forced to tap their daughters' college savings accounts for emergency money. In the interim, the premium on Beth's employer-provided family health insurance rose to $1,000 per month, up from $800. The Faietas were behind on their own mortgage. While they saved $4,000 a month when they sold one of their properties, they still owe more than $18,000 in taxes on their properties and homeowner's insurance bills of more than $5,000.

Like millions swamped by the housing crisis, the Faietas eventually sold their Bonita Springs house for $222,000, losing $60,000 of the $100,000 they put down on it. They still owe one bank $130,000 on another home they sold "short" and were paying it back $50 a month. "Obviously, we can't afford to pay it back," Beth said in late 2008. One saving grace, she noted, is that her hair-extension business was still doing pretty well, despite the closing of fifteen hair salons in recent months.

By early 2009, relieved of some of the stress of sitting on money-losing properties, the Faietas were nearly back on their feet again. "I can see the light at the end of the tunnel," Fabrizio told me. "We've freed up so much money [from the properties] that we're able to pay off our credit cards, cut them up, and throw them in the trash. We're going to be living within our means."

While makeovers, status, entrepreneurship, and upward mobility may remain immutable parts of the American character, we need to get beyond this myth that homeownership is a durable and guaranteed investment in the American dream. For millions, it's been a dangerous fallacy. Untold numbers of mortgages were simply scams; thousands of mortgage-fraud investigations are continuing. The FBI and federal prosecutors have probed more than fourteen hundred mortgage fraud cases involving nineteen companies. More than four hundred people have been indicted, and there may have been more than fifty thousand cases of mortgage fraud in 2007 and thirty-seven thousand the year before.

The ownership society is fractured, but the U.S. housing market will recover over time. Yet there will be no sustainable growth in home sales unless the underlying cost and environmental impact of building and developing drops significantly and tax burdens are spread out more equitably to fund local public services. One of the primary causes of the housing bust was that homes cost too much to begin with, forcing Americans to take desperate measures—getting subprime loans, lying on loan applications—to secure financing. Everyone, from the southern Californian desperate for a tiny starter home to Wall Street billionaires, was complicit in this crisis.

The Obama administration's housing bailout and stimulus plans will help, as will the eventual resolution of bank-insolvency issues. A most promising development is that nearly $40 billion will be spent on energy and green infrastructure funding through the stimulus program (see my book *The Audacity of Help,* Bloomberg Press, 2009, for more details). Everything from tax credits for home alternative energy appliances (solar, wind, geothermal, etc.) to large-scale expenditures for electrical grid modernization will all move America toward a green, sustainable economy. Moreover, this environmentally oriented spending will create millions of jobs, particularly in the construction trades, where more than 800,000 have become jobless since the end of the housing boom in 2006. If pursued aggressively by an ongoing private and public sector partnership, the reinvention of American homes and communities can lead to a boom in investment, employment, and prosperity akin to the information revolution of the past twenty years.

The future of the American middle class—not to mention the health of the planet—is at stake. Building lower-cost, energy-efficient homes in sustainable developments and cities that reduce resource and transportation costs is a start. Doubtless it will take tremendous political will, better designs, enlightened building techniques, more responsive planning, and progressive legislation to enact a new paradigm over the next several years. No matter how much the Obama recovery program affects the short-term state of the mortgage and housing markets, this transformation will not come easy because the status quo on how to develop, build, and create communities needs to change in profound ways. We have to abandon the cul-de-sac mentality and return to the time-honored concept of an American community that can achieve the improbable for the common good over several generations.

Changing course will involve some major cultural soul searching. These mistakes of the housing debacle will cost us trillions and may burden several generations of Americans with debt and create long-standing difficulties in obtaining credit and buying homes. Only one thing is certain: The age of froth is long over. It's time for reckoning and renewal.

—J.F.W.

# Notes

## Introduction
### The Foundation Cracks

The inspiration for the opening to this chapter was a tour of the Alhambra in Granada, Spain, on August 8, 2007, just when the sub-prime and mortgage securities crisis started to ravage credit and stock markets in the United States and abroad. Background history on this magnificent palace complex and the rich history of southern Spain came from Chris Lowney's *A Vanished World: Muslims, Christians, and Jews in Medieval Spain* (Oxford University Press, 2006); Washington Irving's *The Alhambra* (Filiquarian Publishing, 2007); Maria Rosa Menocal's *The Ornament of the World: How Muslims, Jews and Christians Created a Culture of Tolerance in Medieval Spain* (Back Bay Books, 2002); and Robert Irwin's *The Alhambra* (Profile Books, 2005).

The phrase "A man's home is his castle" dates to 1581, according to www.phrases.org.

News accounts that form the basis for the housing crisis narrative came primarily from Bloomberg News; the *Washington Post*, "How HUD Mortgage Policy Fed the Crisis," by Carol Leonnig, June 10, 2008; the *Los Angeles Times*; the *New York Times*, "Housing Woes in U.S. Spread Around the Globe," by Mark Landler, April 14, 2008; *BusinessWeek*, "The Next Real Estate Crisis," by Prashant Gopal, June 5, 2008; the *Wall Street Journal*,

"Why a Housing Bailout Won't Help," by Holman Jenkins Jr., May 21, 2008; *USA Today*, "Cities Suing Lenders in Strategy Against Foreclosures," by Donna Leinwand, May 16, 2008; cnnmoney.com, "Where Home Prices are Headed Next," May 7, 2008; and the Associated Press.

Southern California home-price trends were from the *Los Angeles Times*, "Southern California's Median Home Price Drops Below $300,000," by Peter Hong, December 17, 2008. Also cited were figures from the *New York Times* graphic "Where Homes are Worth Less Than the Mortgage," November 11, 2008; "States Paint a Grim Picture, Ask for Help," by Christopher Cooper and Brad Haynes, the *Wall Street Journal*, December 2, 2008; and "Program Targets Consumer Spending, Mortgage Rates," by Howard Schneider, the *Washington Post*, November 25, 2008.

Figures on foreclosures were from RealtyTrac, based in Irvine, California. Housing price indexes were from the S&P/Case-Shiller home price index (www.macromarkets.com) and the National Association of Realtors (www.realtor.org). The Federal Reserve Board (www.federalreserve.gov) was my source on home-equity valuations as was James Surowiecki's "Home Economics," the *New Yorker*, March 10, 2008. I also relied upon "Sources and Uses of Equity Extracted from Homes," by Alan Greenspan and James Kennedy, March 2007, www.federalreserve.gov/pubs/feds/2007/200720/index.html, which I call "the Greenspan study" in future chapters; and "Stocks Off $2.1 Trillion This Year," by Adam Shell, *USA Today*, July 1, 2008.

My primary source on the growing unaffordability of American homes (in this chapter and throughout the book) was Harvard University's Joint Center for Housing Studies' *The State of the Nation's Housing 2007* (referred to hereafter as "The Harvard Study"), www.jchs.harvard.edu/publications/markets/son2007/index.htm. Also noted was John Cassidy's "The Minsky Moment," from the *New Yorker*, February 4, 2008, citing Frederic Mishkin. The U.S. Census Bureau's "Who Could Afford to Buy a Home in 2002?" July 2007, also provided some background. Other research was culled from statistics issued by the National Association of Realtors, the Federal Reserve, and *InvestmentNews*.

A report, "From Middle to Shaky Ground: The Economic Decline of America's Middle Class, 2000–2006," by Demos, the New York-based think tank, and the Institute for Assets and Social Policy (IASP) at Brandeis University, examining the financial security of the middle class was issued November 19, 2008.

## PART 1  A Dream Gone Bad

## Chapter 1  False Economics
### American Dreamers in the Sunshine State

My stay in Florida in February 2007 included trips to Orlando and Kissimmee for the International Builders' Show, where I toured the "New American Home"; southern Dade County; the Tampa–St. Petersburg area; the Everglades and Big Cypress Swamp; the Fort Myers–Naples area (Bonita Springs and the Faietas' rental property is in between those two cities); and Key West. I drove the entire length of the state—and back.

Daniel McGinn's *House Lust* (Doubleday, 2008) and *Newsweek* articles provided essential background for understanding the American obsession with seeking status through housing.

My comparison of the relative performances of different asset classes is from the *Ibbotson SBBI 2008 Classic Yearbook* (Morningstar, 2008). Other housing background data are from Kathleen Howley's numerous fine dispatches from Bloomberg News, the Naples Area Board of Realtors, the National Association of Realtors, and real estate agent Douglas Brunner of Downing-Frye Realty, www.douglasbrunner.com.

Data on speculation, or "flipping," activity were provided by Mike Ela of www.homesmartreports.com, a specialized service in San Juan Capistrano, California, that measures "collateral risk" in housing markets. Foreclosure data were from RealtyTrac.

Other background included "Is Florida Over?" by Conor Dougherty, the *Wall Street Journal*, September 30, 2007; and "This Is the Sound of a Bursting Bubble," by Peter Goodman, the *New York Times*, December 23, 2007.

The Faietas were also featured in a 2007 column of mine for Bloomberg News as were other subjects in this book that I have since expanded on considerably.

## Chapter 2   Origins of a Dream

My impressions of Williamsburg, Jefferson, and Monticello were from a June 2006 visit to Virginia's Colonial Williamsburg, Jamestown, and Charlottesville.

Supplementary materials included the *Official Guide to Colonial Williamsburg*, by Michael Olmert and Suzanne Coffman (Colonial Williamsburg Foundation, 1998); *American Creation*, by Joseph Ellis (Knopf, 2007); *Thomas Jefferson: A Life*, by Willard Sterne Randall (Henry Holt, 1993); *Jefferson and Monticello: The Biography of a Builder*, by Jack McLaughlin (Henry Holt, 1988); *The Worlds of Thomas Jefferson at Monticello*, by Susan Stein (Harry Abrams in association with the Jefferson Foundation Memorial Foundation, 1993); *Jefferson: Writings* (Library of America, 1984); *Jefferson's Great Gamble: The Remarkable Story of Jefferson, Napoleon and the Men Behind the Louisiana Purchase* (Sourcebooks, 2003); and Calvin Jillson's *Pursuing the American Dream* (University Press of Kansas, 2004). Nathaniel Philbrick's *Mayflower: A Story of Courage, Community, and War* (Viking Adult, 2006) provided insights into the founding of the Massachusetts Bay Colony.

John Locke's views on property are best discovered in his *Second Treatise Concerning Civil Government* first published in 1690.

I quoted Ruskin from John Batchelor's *John Ruskin: A Life* (Carroll & Graf Publishers, 2000) and from his timeless *The Stones of Venice*, edited by J. G. Links (Da Capo Press, 1960)

The McDonough quote was from a personal interview with the architect at the National Association of Home Builders' Green Building conference in St. Louis on March 26, 2007.

My reference to the origin of the cathedral arch is from *Chartres: Sacred Geometry, Sacred Space,* by Gordon Strachan (Floris Books, 2003).

Catherine Beecher's *A Treatise on Domestic Economy, for the Use of Young Ladies at Home, and at School* (Marsh, Capen, Lyon, and Webb, 1841) illuminated my understanding of homemaking during the pre-modern period as did Merritt Ierley's *Open House: A Guided Tour of the American Home 1637–present* (Henry Holt, 1999); Jonathan Hale's *The Old Way of Seeing* (Houghton Mifflin, 1994); and Andrew Jackson Downing's *Cottage Residences; or a Series of Rural Cottages and Cottage-Villas, and their Gardens and Grounds adapted to North America* (Wiley and Putnam, 1856).

On the history of suburbia and Wright's influence, I relied upon Robert Fishman's *Bourgeois Utopias* (Basic Books, 1987); Kenneth Jackson's comprehensive *Crabgrass Frontier* (Oxford University Press, 1985); Jim Cullen's *The American Dream: A Short History of an Idea That Shaped a Nation* (Oxford University Press, 2004); William Hudnut's *Halfway to Everywhere: A Portrait of America's First-Tier Suburbs* (Urban Land Institute, 2004), cited hereafter as *Halfway*; and *American Dreamscape: The Pursuit of Happiness in Postwar Suburbia,* by Tom Martinson (Carroll & Graf Publishers, 2000).

My knowledge of Riverside comes from friends I know who have lived there for more than thirty years; a June 2007 tour; the booklet *Riverside: A Village in a Park* (Frederick Law Olmsted Society of Riverside, 1970); Witold Rybczynski's biography, *A Clearing in the Distance: Frederick Law Olmsted and America in the 19th Century* (Scribner, 1999); Victoria Post Ranney's *Olmsted in Chicago* (Open Parks Project, 1972); and Olmsted's letters.

## Chapter 3   How Debt Addiction Fed a Housing Crisis

I have cited Robert Shiller and his research numerous times in my Bloomberg News column. I did a telephone interview with him on March 2, 2008. His paper, "Understanding Recent Trends in House Prices and Home Ownership," presented at the 2007 Jackson Hole Symposium, details his extensive study of the home-price bubble. Essential

Shiller reading is to be found in the second edition of his *Irrational Exuberance* (Princeton University Press, 2005). His oft-quoted long-term rate of return for housing is cited in this book, although it's disputed by other academics. Also helpful was an interview he did with Jason Zweig, "Shiller Mr. Worst-Case Scenario," posted on cnnmoney.com on July 6, 2007.

The Paul O'Neill quote is from a *New York Times* magazine interview "Market Leader," conducted by Deborah Solomon in the March 30, 2008, issue. Greenspan's speeches are posted on www.federalreserve.gov as is the "Greenspan paper" on home equity, "Sources and Uses of Home Equity Extracted from Homes," cited later in the chapter. A notable critique of Greenspan is presented in William Fleckenstein and Frederick Sheehan's *Greenspan's Bubbles: The Age of Ignorance at the Federal Reserve* (McGraw-Hill Books, 2008). I also relied upon an interview Fleckenstein gave to *Registered Rep*, for its April 2008 issue, and Charles Morris's *Trillion Dollar Meltdown* (PublicAffairs, 2008).

Jacob Hacker provides a deft overview of middle-class Americans losing economic ground in *The Great Risk Shift: The Assault on American Jobs, Families, Health Care and Retirement and How You Can Fight Back* (Oxford University Press, 2006). My figures on American retirement assets are from two papers by James Poterba, Steven Venti, and David Wise. They are "Rise of 401(k) Plans, Lifetime Earnings, and Wealth at Retirement" and "New Estimates of the Future Path of 401(k) Assets." Both were published by the National Bureau of Economic Research (www.nber.org). The decline in participants in defined-benefit pension plans is from EBRI's Fast Facts, February 1, 2007 (www.ebri.org). The relative returns on several assets were from Ibbotson Associates.

Health insurance coverage statistics are from the Henry J. Kaiser Family Foundation (www.kff.org). To track the national debt (and who owns it), see www.treasurydirect.gov/NP/BPDLogin?application=np. David Leonhardt's piece, "For Many, A Boom That Wasn't," in the *New York Times*, April 9, 2008, concisely explains why Americans are falling behind the inflation curve. Richard Thaler's research is amusingly summarized in his *Nudge: Improving Decisions About Health, Wealth, and Happiness*, co-authored by Cass Sunstein (Yale University Press, 2008). The consumer price index dipped in the third and fourth quarters of 2008, although medical and college expenses were expected to remain high.

My source on credit-card debt and subprime lending is the nonprofit Center for Responsible Lending (www.responsiblelending.org), most notably their study "The Plastic Safety Net: The Reality Behind Debt in America," from October 12, 2005. Housing debt information is from the *Wall Street Journal*, "The Housing Crisis Is Over," by Cyril Moulle-Berteaux, May 6, 2008. An illuminating study entitled "The Consequences of Mortgage Credit Expansion: Evidence from the 2007 Mortgage Default Crisis," by Atif Mian and Amir Sufi, was published as a working paper by the National Bureau of Economic Research in April 2008. It was also referenced in Chapter 9. Nan Mooney's *(Not) Keeping Up With Our Parents: The Decline of the Professional Middle Class* (Beacon Press, 2008) detailed further fallbacks in middle-class prosperity. Kevin Phillips's *Bad Money: Reckless Finance, Failed Politics, and the Global Crisis of American Capitalism* (Viking Books, 2008) also provided a wealth of statistics and background on American credit and finance.

My principal source on property taxation was the Tax Foundation's special report, "Property Tax Collections Surged with Housing Boom," by Gerald Prante, from October 2006 (www.taxfoundation.org). I also referenced their "State and Local Tax Burdens Hit 25-Year High." I interviewed Ralph Martire of the Center for Tax and Budget Account-ability on March 19, 2008, and referenced his PowerPoint on Illinois tax reform (www.ctbaonline.org).

The Dane County/Wisconsin studies were cited in "Costs of Sprawl: Tired of Property Taxes? Study Shows We Need to Control Sprawl Development to Control Property Tax Growth," from the Sierra Club (www.sierraclub.org/sprawl/articles/cost.asp). Other property-tax infor-mation was cited from "Property-Tax Collections Climb as Home Prices Fall," by Dennis Cauchon, *USA Today*, December 3, 2008. I also refer-enced data from the U.S. Census Bureau's "National Totals of State and Local Tax Revenue by Type of Tax" through the second quarter of 2008 (www.census.gov).

I again quote McGinn from *House Lust* while supporting some of his argument with figures from the National Association of Home Builders (www.nahb.org), from its yearly survey on home size and amenities. Also instructive is the seminal *The Two-Income Trap: Why Middle-Class Mothers and Fathers Are Going Broke*, by Elizabeth Warren and Amelia Warren Tyagi (Basic Books, 2003), written on the cusp of the bubble in 2002.

## Chapter 4   Cul-de-Sac Nation
### Symptoms of a Syndrome

The Bloomberg News piece cited is "Wealth Evaporates as Gas Prices Clobber McMansions," by Rich Miller and Matthew Benjamin, June 9, 2008.

The oil figures are from the International Energy Agency and "Energy Watchdog Warns of Oil-Production Crunch," by Neil King Jr. and Peter Fritsch, the *Wall Street Journal*, May 22, 2008. Additional production data is from www.worldoil.com. The Robert Bryce quote and figures on electricity consumption are from his *Gusher of Lies: The Dangerous Delusions of "Energy Independence"* (Public Affairs, 2008). Also cited is "Price Jolt: Electricity Bills Going Up, Up, Up," by Paul Davidson, *USA Today*, June 16, 2008, and "Power Prices Set to Surge," by Steve Hargreaves, cnnmoney.com, September 12, 2007. The government source on power consumption is the Energy Information Administration in its *Annual Energy Outlook 2008*, www.eia.doe.gov/oiaf/aeo/electricity .html. Also see "States' Battles Over Energy Grow Fiercer with U.S. in a Policy Gridlock," by Felicity Barringer, the *New York Times*, March 20, 2008. Water consumption by utilities is covered in "Trade-Off Looms for Arid U.S. Regions: Water or Power?" by Peter Spotts, the *Christian Science Monitor*, April 17, 2007. Home water consumption is detailed in "A Thirsty Nation," www.lowimpactliving.com.

The U.S. Geological Survey published a "Droughts in Georgia" paper by Nancy L. Barber and Timothy C. Stamey, in October 2000 that details the history of water shortages in the state (http://pubs.usgs .gov/of/2000/0380). For information on Coca-Cola's water usage, see

"Coca-Cola and Water—An Unsustainable Relationship," by Amit Srivastava, March 7, 2006, on www.commondreams.org. For background on the sustainability of the Atlanta metroplex, see James Howard Kunstler's "Atlanta: Does Edge City Have a Future," on www.kunstler .com/excerpt_atlanta.htm, or his series of books beginning with *The Geography of Nowhere: The Rise and Decline of America's Man-Made Landscape* (Free Press, 1994). On general U.S. water problems, refer to the U.S. EPA's "Water Supply and Use in the United States," www .epa.gov/watersense, the "U.S. Drought Monitor," drought.unl.edu/ dm, and the Associated Press report "Much of U.S. Could See a Water Shortage," by Brian Skoloff, October 26, 2007. For excellent background on the Florida water crisis, consult Debbie Salamone's "Florida's Water Crisis," the *Orlando Sentinel*, March 3, 2002, www.geology .wisc.edu/courses/g115/freshwater/orlandowater.html. For Great Lakes water issues, see *The Great Lakes Water Wars*, by Peter Annin (Island Press, 2006). On overall shortages, I referred to "Scientists Warn of U.S. Water Shortages," by Clive Cookson, the *Financial Times*, February 22, 2007, and "Warming Will Exacerbate Global Water Conflicts," by Doug Struck, the *Washington Post*, August 20, 2007. A prime source for water shortage issues is Robert Glennon's *Water Follies: Groundwater Pumping and the Fate of America's Fresh Waters* (Island Press, 2002), and *Water: The Drop of Life*, by Peter Swanson (Northword Press, 2001). For an overview of the arid West, I referred to "Drying of the West," by Robert Kunzig, *National Geographic*, February 2008, and "Water-Starved California Slows Development; Law Requires 20-Year Supply," by Jennifer Steinhauer, the *New York Times*, June 7, 2008. On a May 2008 trip to southern California, I witnessed the beginning of the wildfire season and the imposition of water restrictions.

The key source on infrastructure issues is the report card by the American Society of Civil Engineers (last published in 2005) at www .asce.org/reportcard/2005/page.cfm?id=108. The costs of suburban development are well detailed in Christopher Leinberger's *The Option of Urbanism: Investing in a New American Dream* (Island Press, 2008), which is also cited in Chapters 10 and 11. Also worth reading is "The Costs of Sprawl Revisited" at www.anthonydowns .com/sprawlrevisited.htm.

Driving figures are from "Next Car Debate: Total Miles Driven," by Joseph White, the *Wall Street Journal*, February 5, 2008, and "Not So Free Ride: What Kind of Incentives Might Persuade Americans to Drive Less," by Stephen Dubner and Steven Levitt, the *New York Times* magazine, April 20, 2008.

## Chapter 5   The Spurbing of National Health

On vehicle-related pollution, consult "Asthma, Traffic and Air Pollution," from the Environmental Defense Fund (www.environmental defense.org/page.cfm?tagID=38) and the Natural Resources Defense Council's "Asthma and Air Pollution," (www.nrdc.org/health/effects/fasthma.asp). The Sierra Club also did a report, "Sprawl Harms Our Health," in its Sprawl Report 2001 (www.sierraclub.org/sprawl/report01/health.asp). Commuting facts are from Nick Paumgarten's "There and Back Again," the *New Yorker*, April 16, 2007. I culled a number of articles on sprawl and health from http://cascadiascorecard .typepad.com/sprawl_and_health/sprawl_general/. Smart Growth America (www.smartgrowthamerica.org/healthreportes.html) also compiled a number of public health studies in its "Measuring the Health Effects of Sprawl" report, September 2003. While environmental and limited-growth groups have a vested interest in curbing sprawl, the research they cite is not from their organizations. There's also a large amount of research that I cite from www.newurbanism.org. A Harvard study on childhood obesity is cited in "Children Sicker Now Than in Past, Harvard Report Says," by Angela Zimm, Bloomberg News, June 26, 2007. The figure on cutting carbon emissions by walking is from *Sierra*, March/April 2008. Bernard-Henri Lévy is quoted from his *American Vertigo: Traveling America in the Footsteps of Tocqueville* (Random House, 2006).

## PART 2   Reinventing Home and Community

## Chapter 6   Toward Sustainable Dreams

I interviewed Victor Zaderej on April 24, 2008, and followed up with numerous e-mails. For more information on his "Pura Vida" home, see www.solarhomesus.com. Click on "metrics" to see performance figures.

One of the most complete pieces on homebuilding waste is found in "Life-Cycle Energy, Costs, and Strategies for Improving a Single-Family House," by Gregory Keoleian, Steven Blanchard, and Peter Reppe, the *Journal of Industrial Ecology*, Spring 2000. The background on the Usonian home site is from "Looking for Mr. Wright," *Construction Dimensions*, June 1989. Additional figures on building costs are from the U.S. Census Bureau's (www.census.gov) "Highlights of Annual 2006 Characteristics of New Housing" (www.census.gov/const/www/highanncharac2006.html).

My sources on indoor air quality were the American Lung Association (www.lungusa.org), the National Safety Council (www.nsc.org), and *ScienceDaily*, "Promote Green Buildings for Biggest, Easiest Cuts in North American Carbon Dioxide Emissions," March 18, 2008 (www.sciencedaily.com/releases/2008/03/080313140108.htm).

Details on the New American Home were gleaned from materials from the National Association of Home Builders brochure, 2007 international show, and www.nrel.gov/docs/fy07osti/39426.pdf.

## Chapter 7  Building Smarter

Extensive details on Kaufmann's homes are available at www.mkdarc.com. I first attended the setting of the Smart Home on March 5, 2008, and saw the grand opening on May 7. Both were at Chicago's Museum of Science and Industry during its seventy-fifth-anniversary celebration year. Her work is profiled in the self-published *Prefab Green: The Work of Michelle Kaufmann Designs* (2006).

Most of my research on Burnham, Olmsted, and Insull was originally conducted for and cited in my book *The Merchant of Power: Sam Insull, Thomas Edison, and the Creation of the Modern Metropolis* (Palgrave MacMillan, 2006). I consulted Richard Munson's *From Edison to Enron: The Business of Power and What It Means for the Future of Electricity* (Praeger Publishers, 2005).

I've also referenced *Frank Lloyd Wright: An Autobiography* (Pomegranate Communications, 2005) and "Frank Lloyd Wright and the House

Beautiful" from the *Frank Lloyd Wright Quarterly*, Winter 2006. I also sourced Alan Hess's *Frank Lloyd Wright Mid-Century Modern* (Rizzoli, 2007) and *Uncommon Sense: The Life of Marshall Erdman,* by Doug Moe and Alice D'Alessio (Erdman Foundation, 2003).

I visited Lennar's "Milano at Monterusso" development on April 19, 2007, and cited details from their sales literature (www.lennar.com). As with the other green home examples, I have noted them in my Bloomberg News columns from 2007. Information on the California solar homes program is from www.gosolarcalifornia.org.

Other green builders were cited in *Green Builder* magazine, September 2008.

## Chapter 8   The Near Death of a Suburb

In addition to having grown up near Park Forest, I made several visits from 2006 through 2008 and questioned several of my longtime friends who lived there. I've also consulted records from the village; *America's Original GI Town: Park Forest, Illinois,* by Gregory Randall (Johns Hopkins University Press, 2000); and William Whyte Jr.'s classic *The Organization Man* (Touchstone, 1956). I interviewed village officials Hildy Kingma and Larry Kerestes on March 10, 2008. The "Downtown Park Forest Master Plan," by the Village of Park Forest, was also reviewed. I did a follow-up visit to Park Forest and Chicago Heights on April 6, 2008.

Also cited was "Park Forest Apartment Complex Cleared of Alleged Squatters; 6 Taken into Custody," by Lolly Bowean, the *Chicago Tribune,* August 15, 2008.

My brief history of Aurora is from the city's Web site www.aurorail .org and the electronic version of *The Encyclopedia of Chicago* (Chicago Historical Society/Newberry Library, 2005). Information on Bigelow Homes is from their Web site, www.bigelowhomes.com, and their product literature. I interviewed Perry Bigelow on April 18, 2008.

My figures on shopping malls are from "The Case Against Sprawl," by Al Norman (1999), www.sprawl-busters.com.

## Chapter 9   Reclaiming the Inner City

I first interviewed Angela Hurlock on March 10, 2006, following up with a neighborhood tour on June 19, 2007, and subsequent phone interviews. A brief history of South Chicago was obtained from "Chicago's Southeast Side Tour," www.neiu.edu/~reseller/setourp12.htm. Information on the Claretian Associates is from www.claretianassociates .org. The census profile is from factfinder.census.gov. I also consulted "Improving the Quality of Life in South Chicago," by the Southeast Chicago Development Commission (2000). I referenced the "Final Report of the Zero Energy Homes for Chicago EcoPower Project," prepared by the Environmental Resources Trust, 2005. Other background on South Chicago was obtained from *Rusted Dreams: Hard Times in a Steel Community,* by David Bensman and Roberta Lynch (McGraw-Hill Books, 1987), and *Always Bring a Crowd!: The Story of Frank Lumpkin, Steelworker,* by Beatrice Lumpkin (International Publishers, 1999).

The figures on security in Chicago Public Schools are from "After Killing, Escorts for Chicago Students," by Susan Saulny, the *New York Times,* April 27, 2008. Employment numbers were from the ADP National Employment Report, as cited in *InvestmentNews,* May 5, 2008.

An outline of the South Works development is from www.mccafferyin terests.com.

Affordable housing figures were gleaned from "Crowley Describes Affordable Housing Shortage," by Eugene Lowe, *U.S. Mayor Newspaper,* February 4, 2002, www.mayors.org; "Housing Burden Rising Across America," cnnmoney.com, October 3, 2006; *Halfway* by Hudnut; "Where Did They Go? The Decline of Middle-Income Neighborhoods in Metropolitan America," by Jason Booza, Jackie Cutsinger, and George Galster, The Brookings Institution, June, 2006; the NAHB's "Characteristics of

First-Time Home Buyers," by Elliot Eisenberg, January 23, 2008 (www
.nahb.org); "Cook Tops in Population Loss Among Counties in the U.S.,"
by John McCormick, EPA *Chicago Tribune* online, March 16, 2006, www
.chicagotribune.com; and the Harvard housing study.

I also cited figures from the Center for Housing Policy's (www.nhc
.org) study "Stretched Thin: The Impact of Rising Housing Expenses on
America's Owners and Renters," issued October 8, 2008.

Additional references are from Fareed Zakaria's "The Future of
American Power," *Foreign Affairs*, May/June 2008; Alex Kotlowitz's
"Blocking the Transmission of Violence," the *New York Times* maga-
zine, May 4, 2008; "Crunching the Numbers on Housing Discrimi-
nation," by Aiesha Little, *The Quill*, March 2008; "Lose Homes, Pay
More Tax," the *New York Times*, May 30, 2008; and "Do Subprime
Loans Create Subprime Cities?" by Gregory Squires, the Economic
Policy Institute, www.sharedprosperity.org, February 28, 2008.

Debt figures were from "Mortgage Crisis Dominates Financial Confer-
ence," *CFA News*, January/February 2008; "Steered Wrong: Brokers,
Borrowers, and Subprime Loans," by the Center for Responsible Lend-
ing, April 8, 2008; "Impact of Mortgage Crunch Spreads," by Dave
Carpenter and J. W. Elphinstone, Associated Press, April 29, 2008; and
"Falling Behind: The High Price of Homeownership," by Kimbriell
Kelly and Alden K. Loury, *The Chicago Reporter* (www.chicagoreporter
.com), April 28, 2008.

## Chapter 10    Sustainability and Development
### Bridging the Gap

The core of McDonough's views on industrial ecology are summarized in
his *Cradle to Cradle: Remaking the Way We Make Things*, co-authored
by Michael Braungart (North Point Press, 2002). His talk at Unity
Temple was on September 19, 2007, and was the keynote of a conference entitled "GreenTown," sponsored by Seven Generations Ahead
(www.sevengenerationsahead.org). He is quoted from his speeches and
his PowerPoint presentation.

Arthur Nelson, one of the world's leading urban growth experts, is quoted from "The Next Slum?" by Christopher Leinberger, the *Atlantic*, March 2008. I've also extensively referenced Leinberger's *The Option of Urbanism: Investing in a New American Dream*; "Understanding the Relationship Between Public Health and the Built Environment: A Report Prepared for the LEED-ND Core Committee," by Reid Ewing and Richard Kreutzer, May 2006 (which quotes the U.S. EPA study); and "The Option of Urbanism" (review of Leinberger's book), by Philip Langdon, *New Urban News*, October/November 2007.

John Norquist was interviewed on March 27, 2008, in Chicago. Andres Duany and Elizabeth Plater-Zyberk were interviewed on March 28, 2008, on the day they were to accept the Driehaus Prize. I reference their influential *Suburban Nation: The Rise of Sprawl and the Decline of the American Dream*, co-authored by Jeff Speck (North Point Press, 2000). Other essential sources include Jane Jacobs's *The Death and Life of Great American Cities* (Random House, 1961); *Green Infrastructure: Linking Landscapes and Communities*, by Mark Benedict and Edward McMahon (Island Press, 2006); *The Next American Metropolis*, by Peter Calthorpe (Princeton Architectural Press, 1993); and *Ecological Design*, by Sim Van der Ryn and Stuart Cowan (Island Press, 1995).

The Congress for the New Urbanism's charter and member projects are from www.cnu.org. I also referred to "Energy and Smart Growth: It's About How and Where We Build," Funders' Network for Smart Growth and Livable Communities, 2004; Norquist's *The Wealth of Cities: Revitalizing the Centers of American Life* (Basic Books, 1999); his "Tear it Down! Removing Freeways—Restoring Cities," the Preservation Institute, 2000 (www.preservenet.com/freeways/FreewaysTear.html); "The Coming Demand," Congress for the New Urbanism; "Oklahoma City Swaps Highway for Park," by Dennis Cauchon, *USA Today*, May 15, 2008; "Seeing Green Through Rose-Colored Glasses," by Joseph Valerio, *Chicago Life*, April 6, 2008; "Advancing a Market for Zero-Energy Homes," by Barbara Farhar, *Solar Today*, January/February 2008; and "Public Transportation, Gas Prices, and Climate," Friends of the Earth fact sheet (www.foe.org), June 9, 2008. I use a Leinberger quote ("the beginning of the end of sprawl") from "Suburbs a Mile Too Far for Some," by Jonathan Karp, the *Wall Street Journal*, June 17, 2008.

My information on buying locally and family farming is from www
.foodroutes.org and the Institute for Local Self-Reliance, www.ilsr.org.

More background on New Urbanist projects was gleaned from "Suburbs
Feeling the Pinch As Fuel Prices Soar," by Helen Chernikoff, Reuters,
July 10, 2008, and the Urban Land Institute's 2008 Global Awards for
Excellence Competition (www.uli.org).

## Chapter 11   The Bill Comes Due
### Which Places Will Prosper?

Although I've made countless visits to and toured Taliesin East several
times over the past twenty years, the most recent was June 29, 2008.
The complex, which includes a farm, the Hillside School, and several
outbuildings, is constantly undergoing renovation by Taliesin Preser-
vation (www.taliesinpreservation.org). On the subject of Wright, I've
referred to the fine biography by Meryle Secrest, *Frank Lloyd Wright*
(Knopf, 1992); *Frank Lloyd Wright Collected Writings*, edited by Bruce
Brooks Pfeiffer (Rizzoli, 1992–1995); *About Wright,* by Edgar Tafel
(John Wiley, 1993); *Usonia, New York: Building a Community with
Frank Lloyd Wright*, by Roland Reisley with John Timpane (Princeton
Architectural Press, 2001); Wright's *The Living City* (Horizon Press,
1958); Ada Louise Huxtable's *Frank Lloyd Wright* (Viking, 2004);
"Return to Broadacre City," by James Krohe Jr., *Illinois Issues*, April
2000; "Ahead of the Curve," by Chris Martell, June 1, 2008, the
*Wisconsin State Journal*; and "Broadacre City Project," www.angelfire
.com/crazy3/kamica/broadacre.html.

I referred to Lewis Mumford's *The Culture of Cities* (Harcourt, Brace,
1938) and his *Sticks and Stones: A Study of American Architecture and
Civilization* (Dover, 1955). While Mumford was frequently at odds with
his friend Wright over Wright's diffuse political views, he championed
his architectural philosophy.

My background on Middleton Hills is from www.middletonhills.com
and Duany's quote in Hale's *The Old Way of Seeing*. I toured Veridian's Grandview Commons on April 23, 2008, and conducted a brief

interview with David Simon later that day at the University of Wisconsin seminar that I was moderating. I did a follow-up interview with Simon on May 13, 2008. "A Green Energy Industry Takes Root in California," by Matt Richtel and John Markoff, the *New York Times*, February 1, 2008, was my source on Berkeley's solar-panel rebates.

I interviewed developer Fred Maas of Del Sur (www.delsurliving.com) on March 14, 2008. My source on the land-conservation study was "Helping Developers Go—and *Make*—Green," Applied Ecological Services (www .appliedeco.com).

The community of Civano, Arizona, has meticulously documented its energy and resource consumption with updated reports at www.civano neighbors.com. An independent review of the community was found in "Success Stories: Civano, Arizona," www.smartcommunities.ncat.org/ success/civano.shtml. I also interviewed Bob Small of the Civano Neighborhood Association on March 11, 2008.

I interviewed Walden Reserve's (www.waldenreserve.com) Tom Bray on June 23, 2008. The green building market projection is from McGraw-Hill Construction, as quoted in "Green Dream Home," by Edward Robinson, *Bloomberg Markets*, July 2008. The *Oak Ridge National Laboratory Review [ORNL]*, Vol. 41, No. 1, 2008, gave a brief mention of Walden Reserve. Although I interviewed Christian in Knoxville, his quote is taken from the article "A Glimpse of the Energy Future," *ORNL Review*, Vol. 40, No. 2, 2007.

The Putnam quote is from his *Bowling Alone: The Collapse and Revival of American Community* (Simon & Schuster, 2000), p. 408, an essential read on the breakdown of American civic culture.

The "Places That Will Prosper" section is based on analyzing data from a number of sources. The main government monitor of home prices is the Office of Federal Housing Enterprise Oversight (www.ofheo.gov), the regulator of government-seized mortgage insurance giants Freddie Mac and Fannie Mae; RealtyTrac (www.realtytrac.com), which prepared customized spreadsheets of high-foreclosure areas; The National Association of Realtors

(www.realtor.com); HomeSmart Reports (www.homesmartreports
.com); and the Federal Reserve (www.federalreserve.gov), particu-
larly Ben Bernanke's speech and presentation of heat maps entitled
"Mortgage Delinquencies and Foreclosures," May 5, 2008. I've also
gleaned information from *Boomburbs: The Rise of America's Acciden-
tal Suburbs,* by Robert Lang and Jennifer LeFurgy (The Brookings
Institution, 2007); and Brookings' three-volume *Redefining Urban &
Suburban America: Evidence from 2000 Census,* Bruce Katz and
Robert Lang, editors (2003). Christopher Leinberger's research for
Brookings was also used as background.

In the "Revitalizing" section, the Zakaria quote is from his *Foreign
Affairs* piece (see above). Extensively detailed proposals on produc-
ing jobs are from the "Community Jobs in the Green Economy,"
by the Apollo Alliance (www.apolloalliance.org). I also consulted
*The Great Neighborhood Book,* by Jay Walljasper (New Society
Publishers, 2007); the U.S. Green Building Council (www.usgbc.org);
*Sierra* magazine (Sierra Club); "The Case for Investing in Energy
Productivity," McKinsey & Company, February 2008; *The United
States of Suburbia: How the Suburbs Took Control of America and
What They Plan to Do With It,* by G. Scott Thomas (Prometheus
Books, 1998); "It's Time to Drop the Mortgage Deduction," by John
Berry, Bloomberg News, May 19, 2005; "Households Priced-Out by
Higher House Prices and Interest Rates," NAHB, December 16,
2008; "City Quick to Go Green," by Tracy Swartz, *Redeye* (*Chicago
Tribune*), December 16, 2008; *Sprawl: A Compact History,* by
Robert Bruegmann (University of Chicago Press, 2005); "Stop
Global Warming Cold," (entire issue) *yes!,* Spring 2008; "Building
a Better Bike Lane," by Nancy Keates, the *Wall Street Journal,*
May 4, 2007; "Bloomberg Draws a Blueprint for a Greener City," by
Thomas Lueck, the *New York Times,* April 23, 2007; 'Spooked Buy-
ers' Amid Bad News, Slow Sales," by Bill Cunniff, the *Chicago Sun-
Times,* March 14, 2008 (Norquist quote); "Feds Object to Energy
Smart Local Governance," by A. Siegel, the *Huffington Post,* May 7,
2008; "Retire the Property Tax," by John Brady, the *New York Times,*
December 16, 2007; "Car Crazy," *National Geographic,* May 2008;
and "The Future for Home Prices," by James Hagerty, December 5,
2008, the *Wall Street Journal.*

## Epilogue    Cleaning Up, Moving On

The tallies for the total bailout and its ramifications will vary going forward, but the estimate at the end of 2008 ($8.5 trillion) was compiled by Bloomberg News. The negative equity figures were contained in the *New York Times* table "Where Homes Are Worth Less Than the Mortgage," November 11, 2008.

Background on the multiple lawsuits and mortgage-fraud investigations is from "Lawsuits Accelerate Amid U.S. Housing Crisis," by Nick Carey, Reuters, May 23, 2008; "Illinois Attorney General Madigan Files Lawsuit Against Mortgage Giant Countrywide," a press release from www.illinoisattorneygeneral.gov, June 25, 2008; "Post-Subprime Economy Means Subpar Growth as New Normal in U.S.," by Rich Miller and Matthew Benjamin, Bloomberg News, May 18, 2008; "Economic Misery More Widespread," by Chris Isidore, cnnmoney.com, May 14, 2008; "As the Benefits Slide" (graphic), *InvestmentNews*, May 26, 2008; "The Scars of Losing a Home," by Robert Shiller, the *New York Times*, May 18, 2008; "New Breed of American Emerges in Need of Food," by Richard Wolf, *USA Today*, May 19, 2008; and "The Bubble: How Homeowners, Speculators and Wall Street Dealmakers Rode a Wave of Easy Money with Crippling Consequences," (series) by Alec Klein and Zachary Goldfarb, the *Washington Post*, June 15, 2008.

# Index

# About Bloomberg

BLOOMBERG L.P., founded in 1981, is a global information services, news, and media company. Headquartered in New York, Bloomberg has sales and news operations worldwide.

Serving customers on six continents, Bloomberg, through its wholly-owned susbsidiary Bloomberg Finance L.P., holds a unique position within the financial services industry by providing an unparalleled range of features in a single package known as the Bloomberg Professional® service. By addressing the demand for investment performance and efficiency through an exceptional combination of information, analytic, electronic trading, and straight-through-processing tools, Bloomberg has built a worldwide customer base of corporations, issuers, financial intermediaries, and institutional investors.

Bloomberg News, founded in 1990, provides stories and columns on business, general news, politics, and sports to leading newspapers and magazines throughout the world. Bloomberg Television, a 24-hour business and financial news network, is produced and distributed globally in seven languages. Bloomberg Radio is an international radio network anchored by flagship station Bloomberg 1130 (WBBR-AM) in New York.

In addition to the Bloomberg Press line of books, Bloomberg publishes *Bloomberg Markets* magazine.

To learn more about Bloomberg, call a sales representative at:

| | |
|---|---|
| London: | 144-20-7330-7500 |
| New York: | 11-212-318-2000 |
| Tokyo: | 181-3-3201-8900 |

# About the Author

JOHN F. WASIK is the award-winning author of twelve other books, including the acclaimed *Merchant of Power: Samuel Insull, Thomas Edison and the Creation of the Modern Metropolis* and *The Audacity of Help* (Bloomberg Press). His column for Bloomberg News is seen by readers on five continents. Wasik has won more than fifteen awards for consumer journalism, including the 2008 Lisagor and several from the National Press Club. He speaks extensively and lives with his wife and two daughters in Grayslake, Illinois. For more information on his work, see www.johnwasik.com or his blog, dailywombat.blogspot.com.